Rome and Reunion

Rome and Reunion

FREDERICK C. GRANT

New York OXFORD UNIVERSITY PRESS 1965

Preface

I was asked to write a book on the Vatican Council, where I was an observer for the Anglican Communion, representing the Protestant Episcopal Church in the United States from October 1962 to March 1963. However, there are already several good books on the Council, by writers far more competent than I and more familiar with the inner movements and views of the Roman Catholic Church. "Xavier Rynne" must know the Cardinals by their first names! And surely there are more books to come, perhaps histories on a par with Dom Cuthbert Butler's authoritative account of Vatican I. Furthermore, I was virtually sworn to secrecy, as were all the observers. Every document we received was marked "sub secreto." Pope John reminded us at the opening of the First Session that he hoped we would not confuse observation with journalism.

Instead, what I have undertaken is to explain to ordinary readers how the Christian church came to find itself in its present situation and why an *aggiornamento* or "bringing up to date" is required throughout Christendom if we are ever to reunite. Everyone knows that there was a Reforma-

v

tion in the sixteenth century and that the church divided
soon afterwards. But the deep underlying causes that led to
the disruption—first and far earlier the "schism" between
the East and the West and then the one between the North
and the South—are not widely known or understood. Only
a historical sketch can make this clear. And so I begin with
the fifth century, when the papacy first brought its full
influence to bear upon the West and the North, and then
trace briefly the stages of development leading to the present. Next I go back and discuss the origins of the papacy
and the relation of the papal claims to the New Testament
data. Some readers will not be interested in this chapter
(VIII) and may choose to skip it.

A final chapter deals with the "unfinished business"
before the Council and before the whole Christian church,
the changes that are required and are now vigorously demanded if we are to have, not reunion all at once, but first
of all Christian fellowship, co-operation, good will, and
mutual confidence as brethren in Christ and "members one
of another." Some Christians believe that reunion must
come first, after which all will be well and great results will
follow. But surely—as Pope John pointed out—a renewal
and revitalizing of the church itself must come first, the recovery of a deeper religious and moral passion, with more
personal freedom and responsibility, more mutual respect,
and a much more serious attention to the precepts of the
gospel. Thus prepared, the church can once again face the
problems of society as a whole and take a firmer, more positive, more creative stand against the increasing chaos and
anarchy of our time. The hour has arrived, and the bell is
already striking. Chaos and the ancient Dark are upon us
once more. A new and far deeper level of world-wide law-
lessness than hitherto now threatens to degrade and destroy

all that is sacred, beautiful, humane, and civilized in our society, all that has been achieved in man's long struggle to rise above savagery and barbarism. It is time for the church to rouse itself and resume its ancient mission, proclaiming once more the divine message of peace among the nations, a peace based upon justice and good will. It is still the message of the coming of that Kingdom of Heaven which is someday to descend upon the earth and bring about the fulfillment of man's age-old dream of a better order, a new world "wherein dwelleth righteousness."

I trust it will be understood that the present work is in no sense official, and does not attempt to present a consensus of Anglican thought on the subject—supposing such a consensus exists. Nor does it attempt to meet the requirements of present-day Roman Catholic theology. Instead, it sets forth the view of one person, greatly concerned for Christian co-operation, fellowship, and mutual understanding, for the genuine continuity of the whole Christian church, for a truly historical understanding of the church's past, and especially for the relation of the later history and the present circumstances of the church to its origins as reflected in the New Testament. It is not the papacy that forms the chief obstacle to reunion, but the unhistorical interpretation of the papacy and its origins. This book is meant to show the real importance of the papacy, and to suggest a pragmatic (rather than an exegetical) basis for considering its function in the life of the whole Christian church. The possibilities implied in this principle, for the future course of reunion, would seem to be obvious.

Contents

I Introduction: The Main Obstacle to Reunion   3

II The Beginning of the Papal Primacy: The Fifth Century   30

III The "Dark" Ages: 500-900   49

IV The Papacy at the Height of Its Power: 900-1300   69

V The Renaissance: 1300-1500   92

VI Reformation and Counter Reformation: 1500-1700   106

VII Since 1700   126

VIII The Origin of the Papacy   145

IX Unfinished Business of the Vatican Council   165

Rome and Reunion

Abbreviations

Bettenson = Henry Bettenson, *Documents of the Christian Church*, New York, Oxford University Press, 2d ed., 1963.

Cross = F. L. Cross, *The Oxford Dictionary of the Christian Church*, New York, Oxford University Press, 1957.

de Journel = M. J. Rouët de Journel, S. J., *Enchiridion Patristicum*, New York, Herder, 22d ed., 1962.

Denzinger = Henricus Denzinger, *Enchiridion Symbolorum*, New York, Herder, 32d ed., 1963.

Heussi = Karl Heussi, *Kompendium der Kirchengeschichte*, Tübingen, Mohr, 12th ed., 1960.

Mirbt = Carl Mirbt, *Quellen zur Geschichte des Papsttums und des römischen Katholizismus*, Tübingen, Mohr, 4th ed., 1924.

I

Introduction:
The Main Obstacle to Reunion

The ordinary person, the man in the street, even the man in the pew, appears to have a somewhat vague idea of the nature and purpose of the present Vatican Council. It is often referred to as an "ecumenical conference," or as a council assembled to promote "church unity" or "reunion." Part of the difficulty the non-specialist, the non-theologian, has with the title is due to unfamiliarity with the historical background of the Council—a background that covers at least four hundred years, and could be thought to cover a thousand years or even the total history of the Christian church since the first century. He knows that the church is divided into various groups, of which the Roman Catholic Church is the largest, with approximately 500 million adherents. Protestantism has approximately 300 million, and Eastern Orthodoxy about 200 million. The Anglicans, usually listed among the Protestants, number something less than 50 million. Although these figures seem large, the Christian church has not been growing in proportion to the world's population. Whereas in 1900 the total number of Christians was estimated at 34 per cent of the world's population, by

1955 it had declined to 31 per cent.[1] Many experts attribute
this decline, in part at least, to the disunion and rivalry, the
competition and overlapping, of the various Christian groups
and to the effect of this obvious rivalry and internal antagonism upon the rest of the world and even upon members
of the churches themselves.

How did the Christian church come to be thus divided?
What steps, if any, have been taken hitherto to maintain or
recover its unity? What historical factors—political, social,
economic, racial, psychological, even temperamental—have
combined to divide the church and keep it divided? Perhaps
even an elementary sketch of one phase of church history
will be useful in explaining the present situation, in dis-
cussing possible steps toward a restoration of the church's
external unity, and in dealing with the problems that remain.

The great problems that confront the Vatican Council
are not only those involved in the reunion of the church or
the adaptation of Catholic worship to modern needs, but are
those that confront all Christians and all religious men and
women today. Chiefly they center in, and arise from, the
growing revolt against all religion, against the religious motivation of life, the religious understanding of human nature
and its destiny, against the most fundamental of all beliefs—
the belief in God, in the human soul, and in the life to come.
Parallel to and involved in this revolt is the one against Christian morals—or even against morals of any kind worthy of
the name—and the determination to live by whatever standards, or lack of them, suit the individual or the group. The
contempt for law and order and the steadily mounting crime
rate throughout the world measure the spread of this revolt
and its unleashing of barbarian, even savage behavior. So

1. See *Die Religion in Geschichte und Gegenwart*, 3d ed., Vol. I, Tübingen, 1957, col. 1718.

does the unfettered greed and materialism, the naked, animal selfishness that infects much of mankind today.

This world is no longer, if it ever was, a Christian world, even in the Christianized parts of it. Nor does a "Christian" society represent or include the "great" nations of the earth. Nor is it Communism alone that opposes Christianity today; Communism is only one front for a totally materialistic and anti-theistic view of life and a purely scientific interpretation of the meaning of existence. The idea that Christianity has already come to terms with modern science, or has discovered that there is no necessary conflict between science and religion, is only self-delusion. The church has not yet begun to take modern science seriously: it is a global tide of thought that offers itself as a substitute for all the ancient religions and philosophies, and finds the good life in a constant escape from moral and political reality in the realm of "pure research," with no responsibility for its discoveries and with no certain goals but only "the glory of going on."

Confronted with this overwhelming crisis, the church—including all the churches—faces it almost without foresight or preparation. Too often, its program no longer embraces the fundamental education of its adherents so that they can meet the onslaught of materialism in belief and decadent paganism in morals. Speaking generally, the church calmly accepts and adopts current pathological types of art, music, poetry, fiction, and architecture, welcoming them as "modern." Even in its use and interpretation of its own sacred scriptures, the church—still speaking generally, of both Protestantism and Catholicism—is incredibly superficial, and has not yet come to grips with modern biblical research. As a consequence, the churches are once more like sitting ducks before the hunter, not even dimly aware of the approaching crisis or faintly conscious of the vast problems that are now emerging and are destined to dominate the thought of the coming century, or centuries. The thought of the church, both Protestant and Catholic, is far too apologetic, too polemical, defensive, institutional and conceptual, legalistic and juridical, viewing Christianity as an inspired system of theology rather than as a religion centered in a new way of life and promising a new pattern of human existence once the world takes its principles in earnest.

In some areas, it would seem, the church has even begun to abandon its ancient gospel of faith, love, and obedience to the will of God. What has become of Christian ethics in its teaching? Even fifty years ago, a confirmation class was expected to study Christian morals: the Ten Commandments, expounded and applied in the light of the Sermon on the Mount. But all this is now often viewed as "mere moralism," an outlook that only encourages pride and self-assurance. And so, instead of "Thou shalt not steal" and other sound principles, we get brief instructions in "How to follow the church service" or "Why I am not a Baptist" or "a Roman Catholic" or "a Unitarian." Or, on the other hand, we have "the New Morality," with its open avowal of sex perversion as a legitimate "way of life" even for a Christian. All this is incredible—but true. It is surely not only the Roman Catholic Church, the largest in Christendom, that needs a course of "up-dating," but also the rest of us, and Christendom as a whole. The church has fallen on weary, stale, flat, unprofitable times, and appears (in some quarters) to be abandoning its central teaching mission on the very eve of the greatest moral and intellectual test it has ever been required to face. It is to the credit of the Mother Church of Western Christendom that she fully recognizes the situation and the need if the crisis is to be met and overcome.

Not only is Christian ethical teaching neglected; too much

of our current ecumenical discussion or dialogue is being
conducted on the basis of an out-dated biblicism, on the principle of "taking the Bible just as it is." This procedure
is most unfortunate, for a double reason. The antiquated, literalist, fundamentalist view of the Bible is crumbling before our eyes. At the same time, the view supported
by modern biblical research is not only inevitable, if modern
education continues, but is far more promising as a guide
and support to sound and adequate ecumenical views. For
example, the view of Christian tradition as antecedent to the
written New Testament is not only historically sound but
inescapable; and not only inescapable but indispensable to a
satisfactory view of the rise of Christianity, its nature, and
the truth of its teaching. On the other hand, the main
obstacle to Christian reunion is not papal infallibility or
even the papal primacy, which could be adequately defended on historical or pragmatic grounds (see Chapters
II to VII) on the basis of practical needs for centralized
government and administration of the Christian church. The
real obstacle is the violence done to the New Testament in
every attempt to defend the primacy as an institution dating
from the first century and founded by Christ himself. This
unfortunate procedure results from, or is made possible by,
the uncritical views of both history and scripture that have
been inherited from the distant past, not only from the
Middle Ages, but from the Patristic Period at the beginning of the Dark Ages. A new kind of Catholicism, frankly
adopting modern historical and biblical criticism, and com-
bining with it a fresh revival of the Platonic philosophy
which, with its profound spiritual realism, has always been
the "nursing mother" of vital Christian theology, and at the
same time relying more fully than hitherto, since the first
century, upon the direct guidance of the Church by the

Holy Spirit—such a type of Catholicism would open wide the way toward future religious advance and provide a witness to the eternal spiritual and moral truths for want of which our age is slowly but steadily perishing. Such a Catholicism would make unnecessary the "ecumenical movement," and would provide the world with what all men are searching for: a religion pure and undefiled, with power to transform and direct human life in the ways that God intended as part of His cosmic design. The first step, accordingly, must be a fresh view of Christian history, and a clear, scientific, genuinely religious (not merely theological) interpretation of the sacred writings of the Old and New Testaments. Above all, we need a reaffirmation of the ancient Christian principle of taking all history seriously.

Most Christians naturally, and excusably, do not acquaint themselves with the detailed textual criticism of the Bible or its intricate literary analysis. These matters they leave to the experts. But these are indispensable procedures in all thorough study of the Bible. How can we deal with any ancient book if the text is ignored and its variant readings are suppressed? Or how can we explain to modern students the complicated interrelations of the gospels, or the Pauline chronology, or the sources of Acts or the Apocalypse without a careful examination of every minute detail in the sacred volume? And how can anyone use the New Testament as a source for the earliest history of Christianity, or judge the use made of it by others in reconstructing Christian origins, without a detailed and explicit acquaintance with biblical criticism? It is customary for Protestants to charge the Roman Catholic Church with a failure to "teach the Bible." This is true only of the uneducated among the laity. Multitudes of the Roman Catholic laity study the Bible, and those who cannot read have other media of infor-

mation—for example, the pictures, paintings, mosaics, or
windows of churches that tell the Bible story. The interior
of the cathedral at Monreale, above Palermo, is covered
with biblical illustrations. The very floor of the cathedral
at Siena recounts the wars of the Maccabees. But this is not
enough. The inner meaning of the sacred writings must be
made clear. On the other hand, some of the examples of
popular Protestantism are nothing to be proud of. The stir
created by the Bishop of Woolwich's little book, *Honest
to God*, is almost inconceivable, but true. It is almost un-
believable that the disclosure that "God is not *up there*,"
but everywhere, should be shocking. It is like the Russian
astronaut's comment that God and the angels were nowhere
to be seen in outer space. At the Protestant Bible exhibit at
the New York World's Fair, an exhibitor declared that all
the books of the Bible were written in Aramaic, that the
Greek is only a translation, and that the English is only a
translation of a translation. Surely the "open Bible" ought
to produce something better than this—and it does. But unfortunately the requirement of a certain degree of education
is not enforced in some groups, and people are allowed to
begin explaining holy scripture before they have learned
anything about it.

Among the ways of classifying human beings, one is
assuredly relevant when we undertake to deal with religion:
it is the broad distinction between those who take history
seriously and those who do not; between those for whom
historical criticism is important and those for whom it is not;
between those for whom the past is real and those for whom
it is imaginary, a realm of fiction or fancy, where anything
may or may not have happened; between those who trust
the results of historical research and those who feel free to
brush them aside as unimportant or even dangerous. This

classification not only covers the various religions of mankind, or the sects within any one religion; it runs throughout the whole of the religious life of mankind. There are
not only religions, but groups within the various religions,
that are either preponderantly historically-minded or mainly
a-historical in outlook. Of course, no one is entitled to pass
a sweeping judgment upon either a church or an individual.
One can never say, "This man's religion is vain," or say that
it is wholly, or merely, historical; nor can one say that it is
simply a-historical, aesthetic, ceremonious, theological, dogmatic, or the like.

For many persons in all religions and in all churches the
essential matter is worship, contact and communion with a
present spiritual reality, regardless of past history, origins,
antecedents, or earlier forms; for others, the main interest
is the artistic expression of religion in sculpture, painting,
architecture, or in drama, music, pageantry, and song. The
historical validation of the subject matter is, for them,
wholly irrelevant, even an intrusion and a nuisance, and
they cannot understand those who insist upon bringing up
such questions. For still others the ultimate reality is metaphysical, and the pathway leads through a labyrinth of
philosophical categories—essences, ontological realities like
"nature," "person," "substance," divine "will," and so on—
where safety and security lie in following the Ariadne's
thread of pure logic. And for still others the judicial element
is supreme. It not only decrees and controls behavior appropriate to the common creed but even determines what must
or must not be believed—as if one could really "believe" in
God or in Purgatory or in papal infallibility in response to
an authoritative command. Faith is something more than
assent, or subscription. On the other hand, for those who
take history seriously, all these other approaches to religion,

however legitimate they may be for those who accept or maintain them, are quite impossible, unless combined with serious and honest historical examination. It is a matter of conscience, and no amount of toleration, good fellowship, or "ecumenical spirit" can release them from their prior adherence to the truth as they conceive or apprehend it. To disregard the facts of history, once these are ascertained, or to ignore the statements of ancient records, once these are understood, would be to affirm "the lie in the soul," which was Plato's term for the unforgivable sin (*Republic* 2.382; cf. *Philebus* 39).

It is not in the least probable that those who see otherwise, those for whom historical obligations or realities are more or less irrelevant, will be able to comprehend what animates their stubbornly recalcitrant brethren. It would be like trying to persuade one who adheres to classical forms of music that the disregard of all form may be beautiful or satisfying. Here lies a greater obstacle to Christian reunion than any of the commonly recognized barriers, which easily fall under the condemnation either of pride, ignorance, self-will, or disobedience, or of apostasy, heresy, or schism. The difficulty lies far deeper: superficial exegesis of holy scripture, and an unhistorical account of the rise and early history of Christianity, are not matters that can be ignored and over-looked, even for the sake of Christian fellowship or the external reunion of the church. Such efforts need not be dismissed with animosity. A polemical treatment is completely useless, for it lacks any common ground, any fulcrum for leverage. It is as if one were to build a bridge in mid-air with no approach at either end; or, better, as if one built a bridge from both ends but with middle spans that not only did not meet but actually by-passed each other. Those churches for whom sacred history is beyond the reach of criticism or of scientific investigation will not be able to converse intelligibly with those for whom both holy scripture and ancient history are subjects for careful research with the best available means of investigation.

It is sometimes said that biblical study will draw the churches together. This would be ideal, if practicable. But it is an ideal that still lies in the distant future. Both on the Protestant side and on the Roman Catholic, and also on the side of Orthodoxy and of Anglicanism, there are those who simply do not take modern biblical research seriously. For example, many Christians place the Synoptic Gospels and the Gospel of John side by side and weave them together as if they were one fabric, with no distinction between their divergent points of view, aims, underlying traditions, or earlier sources. Even their distinct and distinguishing vocabularies are combined, and also the theological ideas they presuppose and the history of primitive Christian doctrine they reflect. Such a view of exegesis and interpretation is quite hopeless as a contribution to ecumenical understanding. If this attitude prevails, it will be the end of real *rapprochement* between any but fundamentalists on both sides. And they may not agree either.

Consider, for example, the promise to Peter in Matthew 16.18f. It is not interpreted in John, as some of the other Synoptic sayings are interpreted; it is not even mentioned or presupposed. Nor does it appear in any other gospel. Nor is it presupposed in the Acts of the Apostles. A wholly different account is found in John 1.40-42, where Simon's name is changed to Cephas "which means Peter," but with no explanation of its significance. Perhaps, as C. K. Barrett suggests in his *Commentary on John* (1955), the author of the Fourth Gospel realized that "Peter's subsequent career" did not bear out either interpretation, Matthew's or his own.

Presumably "Peter" had been the Apostle's Greek name for a long time (double names, Semitic and Greek, were common in Palestine), and hence was not given him by Jesus on any one single identifiable occasion. If so, Jesus simply stressed the meaning of the name ("rock"), recognizing its significance as borne by the one who would be the leader of the disciples. But John has no hint of Peter's office as the "foundation" of the church, nor has any other writer in the New Testament. Not even Matthew offers any such hint, if properly interpreted: the "foundation" was surely the divine revelation that lay behind Peter's words acknowledging Jesus' Messiahship, not the person of Peter himself. The latter idea completely contravenes New Testament teaching: "Other foundation can no man lay than that [which] is laid, which is Jesus Christ" (1 Cor. 3.11). Paul's words read almost like a repudiation of the later claim made for Peter. So does the expostulatory opening of the first epistle to the Corinthians as a whole; the slogan "I belong to Cephas" (1.12) can only mean the Petrine party.

These are questions that cannot be ignored if we take the Bible in earnest. No theory of a secret tradition, accompanying the New Testament writings and providing their proper interpretation, can explain them away. There is no early evidence for any such hermeneutical tradition. It is no answer to these questions to heap ridicule upon "higher criticism." That only brings into disrepute all biblical research and matches the diatribes of unbelievers.

Much of the popular interpretation of the Bible, both Catholic and Protestant, is really traditional, and has been handed down from the ancient pre-critical period—not from the Middle Ages but from the Church Fathers. Even today courage is required on the part of those brave spirits who are seeking to free themselves from the wearisome

burden of antiquity and to understand the scriptures in
their true original sense, as disclosed by modern research.
Much of the traditional interpretation is literary and allu-
sive; much of it is quaint and archaic and imaginative, like
poetic inscriptions in all ages. It can be called exegesis only
by forcing the term and resorting to allegorical interpretation or "typology." This is really *eisēgēsis*, not *exēgēsis*, a
reading in, not a reading out. Take, for example, the scripture texts inscribed upon the votive column of Pope Pius IX,
commemorating the Decree (in 1854) on the Immaculate
Conception of the Blessed Virgin Mary; the column stands
in the Piazza di Spagna at Rome, just east of the foot of the
Spanish Steps. The prophets who foretold the Immaculate
Conception were David, Moses, Ezekiel, and Isaiah. *Teste
David:* (Psalm 45.4) *Sanctificavit tabernaculum suum Altis-
simus* ("The Most High has sanctified thy tabernacle"—
the new Roman Psalter would be even more appropriate,
sanctissimum tabernaculum Altissimi, "the most holy tabernacle of the Most High"). *Teste Moyses:* (Genesis 3.15)
Inimicitia inter te et mulierem ("I will put enmity between
you and the woman"). *Teste Ezechiel:* (44.2) *Porta haec
clausa erit* ("This gate shall remain closed"). *Teste Isaias:*
(7.14) *Ecce Virgo concipiet et pariet filium* ("Behold, a
Virgin shall conceive and bear a Son"). Similar fanciful
use of the Old Testament is to be found all over the world
of Catholic and early Protestant art, devotion, hymnology.
The old commentary on the Psalms by J. M. Neale and
R. F. Littledale (4 vols., 1860-74, based on patristic and
mediaeval exegesis) is full of this kind of interpretation,
which sought to find clues to the secret meanings of the
Old Testament in the teachings and even the narratives of
the New. The exquisite drawings in the beautiful Missal
published by Friedrich Pustet (Regensburg, 1930) provide

examples: Exodus 17.11 illustrates the Crucifixion. "Whenever Moses held up his hands, Israel prevailed"; 1 Kings
16.12 foretold the timbers of the cross: the widow of Zare-
phath said, "I am gathering two pieces of wood." It is like
the famous painting in which the Boy Jesus stands, with
arms extended, in the doorway of Joseph's carpenter shop;
the sunlight behind him leaves the shadow of a cross upon
the floor of the shop. This is poetry, fancy, imagination,
and is not to be discouraged unless it be insisted that the
original meaning of scripture is set forth in these interpretations. Then we must protest.

The same artistic, imaginative, rather than scientific approach, to still other texts, for example the "Petrine" passages in the New Testament, resulted in the mediaeval
theological or ecclesiological exegesis and the cumulative
argument for the papal claims. On a historical view, it is
often impossible to trace the later "traditional" interpretation of these passages to their period of origin. True, there
were valiant defenders of tradition in the early period—for
example, Papias of Hierapolis (ca. 135), who preferred "the
living and abiding voice" of tradition to the written records,[2]
and before him Clement of Rome (ca. 98), who appealed
to his readers in Corinth (*First Epistle* 7.2) in these words:
"Let us abandon vain and empty conjectures and come to
the famous and revered rule of our tradition." [3] But to what
does this refer? To historical records, or to exegesis?

Most of us scarcely realize how sketchy and fragmentary
are the records of the early church. Irenaeus of Lyons (ca.
185) lists the bishops of Rome down to his own days.[4] The
list begins with Linus, not Peter. "After the founding of

2. Bettenson, p. 38.
3. Cf. Bettenson, pp. 88f.
4. Cf. Bettenson, pp. 96-9.

the church in Rome by Peter and Paul," he says, "their
successors were: Linus, Anacletus, Clement, Euaristus, Alexander, Sixtus, Telesphorus, Hyginus, Pius, Anicetus, Soter,
Eleutherus." The list is obviously traditional, though the
dates later assigned to the reigns of these twelve early
bishops are quite uncertain. Irenaeus must surely have
known personally the last four, beginning with Pius, about
A.D. 150. The early church in Rome, and elsewhere, does
not seem to have been much interested in keeping records.
In fact, it is probably not until we reach Anterus (A.D.
235-6) that we have any assurance of exact dates. And this
is about all we know of the early Roman church—the names
in this list, and the *First Epistle* of Clement, and *The Shep-
herd* of Hermas, none of which throw much light on the
history of the church in the capital. But the limitation of
our knowledge does not mean that the Roman church was
not the most conspicuous and influential of all Christian
churches. Even in the first century it was viewed as the
most outstanding of all, obviously because it was the church
in the capital of the world as well as of the Roman Empire;
and it was soon the largest, the most influential, perhaps the
richest church in the world: its concern for the welfare of
other churches had been notable from the outset. The wealth
and power, the splendor and magnificence of Rome in the
first and second centuries is almost beyond description. It
was the universal city, the capital of all mankind (as many
supposed), destined to be the everlasting mistress and queen
of the divinely appointed world empire. Naturally, the
church shared this earthly eminence, in the minds of all
Christians. Moreover, it was well known that the church in
Rome preserved the true faith, uncontaminated by Gnostic
errors and perversions of the fundamental Christian teaching; hence, according to Irenaeus (3.3.1), "It is necessary for

every church to be in agreement with this church because of
its outstanding pre-eminence [*potentiorem principalitatem*,
which some scholars have taken to mean its age, its early
foundation, prior to other churches in the West]—that is,
[it is necessary] for all the faithful everywhere, since it
preserves the tradition which has come down from the
Apostles." [5] Thus the way in which the early Church Fathers
referred to it clearly implies its importance. But all this was
probably the consequence of natural causes and circumstances, its location, its date of founding, its close association
with the center of the empire, and its loyalty to the traditional faith, not the result of some prerogative conferred
upon Peter and his successors.

In fact, it is only a probability, not a certainty, that Peter
was martyred in Rome; some scholars doubt that he ever
saw Rome—the reference to "another place," in Acts 12.17,
may be understood to mean some town in Palestine, or even
in Judaea. In Acts 15.7 he is still (or again) in Jerusalem.
Nor was he present at the commissioning of Paul and
Barnabas at Antioch when they set forth on Paul's First
Missionary Journey (Acts 13.1-3). His presence there, described in Galatians 2.11-21, must have been considerably
later; and his assumed presence in Corinth (in 1 Cor. 1.12,
etc.) is not absolutely certain: the existence of partisans of
Peter in Corinth does not require his presence there. Moreover, the fact that the position credited to him in Matthew
16.17-19 (as usually interpreted) is not reflected anywhere
else in the New Testament, or in the earliest Christian literature outside the New Testament, destroys the theory that
the Petrine primacy was part of the church's tradition from
the beginning. But it was this unfortunate silence that
opened the way to fanciful exegesis—or eisegesis—which

5. Bettenson, pp. 96f.

steadily grew as later "tradition" developed. As we shall
see, it was not Peter but Paul who said that upon him lay
the burden, the "daily pressure" of "anxiety for all the
churches" (2 Cor. 11.28). If only Peter had said this, how
often it would have been quoted!

The interpretation of the Bible "in its plain and literal
sense" is a fruit of the Protestant Reformation, just as once,
long before, allegorism had been the fruit of the Alexandrian
theology, its methods of interpretation having been taken
over from Philo Judaeus. Modern fundamentalist literalism
is also a fruit of the Reformation, literalism now being
pushed to an extreme, far beyond the original intention of
the biblical writers. But the poetic, artistic, imaginative interpretation likewise lends itself to literalism, and to a juridical,
legal, constitutional kind of literalism that is equally foreign
to the original meaning. When theologians plead, as some
do, for a biblical theology which shall be, not a partition
or dissection of the Bible into its component sources or
levels of tradition or types of religious thought, but an
integrated and fully synthetic structure, based upon the
"unity" of holy scripture, they are really asking that historical exegesis and the results of two centuries of biblical research be abandoned. What they are asking for is a system
of "biblical" theology as compact, consistent, and logically
watertight as the *Summa* of St. Thomas or the *Institutes*
of John Calvin or the *Longer Catechism*.

This is the point at which serious difficulty will arise
when Roman Catholic and Protestant Christians compare
notes and consider prospects for reunion. Many of us on
both sides need a truer, sounder view of the nature of holy
scripture, and of the possibilities, and the limits, of scholarly
exegesis and of theological interpretation. It may turn out

in the end that the Bible simply cannot be squeezed into a set of dogmatic categories, and that no one airtight system of theology ever was or could be presupposed in the sacred writings. It may be that it was not the purpose of divine revelation to affirm authoritatively a body of conceptual statements, all as neatly intergeared as a collection of precision-milled parts in a delicate instrument, say a watch or a computer. It may very well be that much of the Bible— New Testament as well as Old—is pure poetry, calling for poetic interpretation rather than legal or dogmatic interpretation. As Ernst Haenchen says in his great commentary on the Acts of the Apostles (Göttingen, 1956), only a poet can interpret poetry. The prophets were clearly poets— anyone can recognize this when their writings are arranged in verse form, as in the new versions, for example, the American Revised Standard Version (1952), or in the beautiful French edition of the Vulgate (Paris, 1938). But the same is true of the New Testament, as seen in the Gospel and Epistles of John in the new *Jerusalem Bible* (Paris, 1955): much of the content of the Gospels is poetic in form, much more even than most of the modern versions indicate. The tradition of the life and teaching of Jesus called for a poetic expression, as is true in much of ancient religious literature and, back of the literature, in ancient oral tradition, especially religious tradition. For many centuries, the poetic embodiment of religious teaching had been common in the Orient, and it was to remain common for centuries to come. But the modern world does not look for poetry. Today, poetry is often viewed as synonymous with nonsense, with exaggeration and extravagance, words being twisted out of their normal meanings and the whole veiled in obscurity, crudity, or even ugliness—totally out of touch with the world of normal experience and of tangible reality.

Whereas, in the realm of the spirit, only poetry can hint or suggest the meanings that pass beyond our full comprehension: "What eye has not seen, nor ear heard, neither has it entered into the heart of man to conceive, things passing knowledge, which God has prepared for those who love Him" (cf. 1 Cor. 2.9). A truer view of the Bible is required, one that will take into full account the form as well as the content of its message. How necessary this is may be inferred from the Encyclical of Pope Pius XII, *Divino afflante Spiritu* (1943),[6] in which he pointed out the difference between Eastern literature and Western, and the necessity of interpreting the figurative language of Oriental writings, including the Bible.

All Christians maintain that the church was founded upon a divine revelation, which began several centuries before the birth of Christ. The record of this revelation is contained in the Bible. And the Bible is the collection of sacred books authorized by the church for use in worship, in teaching, and in the establishment of sound doctrine. This looks like an argument in a circle, but it really is not. The "authorization" was not a simple act of some committee, council, patriarch, or pope. Nor was it an answer to Marcion's canon, which abridged or deleted and revised the New Testament in a Gnostic direction (he had already abandoned the Old Testament as Jewish); nor did the church's canon compete with any other. The selection of the books, like their survival, was the result of long use, first (the Old Testament) in the Jewish synagogue and later (Old Testament and New alike) in the Christian church. These books were found to be "useful for teaching, for reproof, for correction, and for training in righteousness" (see 2 Tim. 3.16). Hence they were studied and read aloud and treas-

6. Denzinger, §§ 3825-31.

ured and expounded through the centuries. Eventually, official lists were drawn up and hedged about with canonical sanction, as other books were proposed for addition to the collection—books that were unworthy of inclusion, such as the fantastic writings of the Gnostics. But the source of the whole body of sacred scripture was use and wont, tradition and memorization and exposition in a religious group. It was no fiat of a judicial or legislative authority that sanctioned the Bible, or its earliest use: the sanction came later, when the process of collection was virtually complete. As Emerson said,

> Out from the heart of Nature rolled
> The burdens of the Bible old.

The books of the Bible were the inspired writings cherished within a living, developing religion. This had been as true of the Old Testament as it was of the New. In fact, the growth and gathering of the New Testament literature was designed to provide a supplement to the Old Testament, now in its Greek form as the Septuagint of the early church. Thus the authority of the Old Testament scriptures was simply taken over from Judaism, along with much else in its worship, customs, theology, biblical exposition, and ideology in general. And the same authority was made to cover the New Testament, when it was added to the Old, to form the "great Bible" of the Christian church—the Bible recognized everywhere in East and West, in Greek and Latin and in the later versions—until the Bible societies in the early nineteenth century began to omit the Apocrypha.[7]

7. On the importance of lectionary use not only for the history of the Canon but also for the translation and interpretation of the Bible in the church, as also earlier in the Jewish synagogue, see my *Translating the Bible*, Edinburgh and New York, 1961.

Far from being an idle debate among theologians, the struggle over scripture and tradition, at Trent, at Vatican I, and now at Vatican II, is crucial and fundamental to the whole position of the church. In his lectures on *The Rise of the Greek Epic*, Gilbert Murray, the eminent classicist, described the Bible as "a traditional book." The truth of this characterization is obvious. The opening chapters of Genesis were transmitted orally for a long time before they were written down—except, perhaps, the great opening prose-poem on the Creation, which may possibly still retain its author's exact formulation and structure. The stories that follow were legends long before they were written down in books. The Law as a whole, i.e. the Torah or Pentateuch, was at first oral and then written. In this respect it closely resembled most of the rest of ancient law. The stories in Judges, Ruth, 1-2 Samuel, 1-2 Kings, 1-2 Chronicles were sagas, legends, folk tales, with occasional reference to the annals of the kingdoms of Israel and Judah. The Samuel cycle and the David cycle are clearly distinguishable within the present cadre of narrative. Ezra and Nehemiah were memoirs, though with reference to traditional material, especially genealogies. The Psalms and Proverbs were probably collections of orally transmitted hymns and wise sayings. The books of the prophets were written. But once we are in the Apocrypha the element of tradition is again recognizable, especially in 1 Esdras, 1-2 Maccabees, Judith, Tobit, Susanna, Bel and the Dragon. This tradition is on different levels, some of it quite historical, much of it legendary or purely fanciful and fictitious. In the New Testament, the gospels are based upon what was originally oral tradition (see Luke 1.1-4), and so is most of the Acts of the Apostles, which is a continuation of the Gospel of Luke, by the same author and following the same methods of composition and editing. The epistles were written works, still substantially as they left their authors' hands, though according to many scholars—and now also according to the results of computer tests, it is reported—the minor Pauline letters were considerably edited. Some parts of the book of Revelation, the Apocalypse of John, were clearly traditional, drawn from the common stock of Jewish and early Christian apocalyptic —the *Jerusalem Bible* credits it to two authors or compilers.

Even after the New Testament was complete, the oral tradition still survived (as we have seen in the case of Papias), and also continued to grow. Tradition was to be preferred to the written testimony of the scriptures, according to some writers: that is to say, preferred to the testimony contained in the new Christian books which were now being added to the Greek translation of the Hebrew Bible with its more ancient "testimonies" and oracles foretelling Christ and the Gospel. After Papias and the "Apostolic Fathers" came the Apologists, and then the Early Church Fathers, all of them contributing to and handing on the growing tradition of interpretation and exegesis, of both the Old Testament and its Christian supplement, which eventually came to be called the "New" Testament. It was a mark of the immense vitality of the early church that this was so. A living religion produces tradition as it sweeps along through history, not a mere *repertorium* of ancient lore but the creation of fresh, newly minted ideas, explanations, and interpretations in sermons, hymns, creeds, and books. This tradition was a continuous stream, each generation adding to the accumulation, some even adding sacred writings which all but matched the standard of the canonical literature: for example, the liturgies, the creeds, or, later on, such works as the *Rule* of St. Benedict [8] or the

8. Bettenson, pp. 161-79.

Imitation of Christ by Thomas à Kempis, based on an earlier
devotional manual of the Brethren of the Common Life.
It is impossible to recognize the existence of tradition prior
to the Bible and then ignore it after the Bible. The church's
very teaching was traditional (see 2 Thess. 2.15; 3.6; 1 Cor.
15.3), antedating the New Testament writings, accompanying them, following and interpreting them. In fact, the two,
scripture and tradition, are inseparable in any *living* religion.
They overlap, and they presuppose each other. Only moribund or totally defunct religions, only dead cults of the
past are subject to anatomical dissection and classification,
with sharp distinctions drawn between the written and the
oral transmission of their sacred teachings, sacred legends,
and sacred histories.

It is a mistake to require a choice between scripture and
tradition, as Protestants do with their insistence upon *sola
scriptura,* or Roman Catholics with their preference for
tradition. In the latter case the Bible is to be interpreted
strictly in accordance with the tradition, though the tradition may not be more than a few centuries old. In the end
the tradition becomes overburdened with new material and
fresh additions. In the light of history, *both* scripture and
tradition are bearers of the sacred deposit—what we may
call "the church's memories"—and also the sacred message
of truth, the gospel of life. One of these must be used to
interpret the other, whenever interpretation is required.
This distinction of course goes back to Judaism, the mother
of Christianity, both Catholic and Protestant; and its sage
wisdom has been justified by its works. The stark literalism
of some rabbinic teachers was matched and counterbalanced
by the free movement of a stream of tradition, theoretically
coming down from Moses and the elders on Mt. Sinai but
refusing to be bound by the dead hand of the past. This also

was the mark of a living religion, adaptable, resilient, facing new situations with courage and freedom, confidence and faith.

Throughout its history, Christianity has been much more than "the religion of a book." It has insisted upon the presence and the continuous activity and power of the Holy Spirit, and also upon the real presence of its exalted Lord, not only in the Eucharist but in every aspect of its life, in missions, in acts of healing and restoration, in forgiveness and the power to cease from sin, in preaching and teaching, in administration and pastoral care, in study and learning, in the life of the saint and in the life of the scholar, in the upholding of the weak and the rescue of the lost. The God of the New Testament is the Living God, even as He is in the Old Testament. Only an arid, sterile rationalism can ignore the continuance of miracles, the reality of special guidance and inspiration, the on-going conversation of God with men through the centuries, the reality of prayer and of "answers" to prayer, all of which are characteristic and perfectly natural in a living religion. If this free growth of faith seems to be more obviously characteristic of Catholicism than of Protestantism, this is due chiefly to its open acknowledgment and expectation among Catholics and to the theological theory that forms the background and supplies the encouragement for such phenomena. But the facts are present in Protestantism as well as in Catholicism, in spite of the overlay of repression and discouragement provided by the traditional Reformation theology, the criticism of Catholic "superstition," and the repressive mood of the more severely intellectual of the sects and denominations.

It is against the foil of this historical phenomenon that the place of holy scripture in religion must be tested and ascertained. It is curious, in a way, that the church ever

required a Bible, or acquired one. Conceivably, the tradition alone and by itself might have sufficed. And it is also
curious that the theory of inspiration (derived chiefly from
the experience of the early Hebrew prophets and from the
religious beliefs of the circumambient Hellenism of the age
following Alexander the Great) ever took hold upon men's
minds in the degree to which it is reflected both in rabbinic
teaching and in patristic theology. The theory of several
different "senses" of holy scripture, all of them valid and
infallible, was a desperate resort in the days before historical criticism had arisen. If the Bible was inspired, every
syllable must contain a meaning, must mean something, not
only as it did long ago but even now; and if this meaning
is not clear and obvious at once, further research (*midrash*,
darashah) must yield something of value. The principle was
as fully believed and practised by the Church Fathers as it
was by the ancient rabbis and by Philo of Alexandria.
Indeed, the line that runs from Philo to Origen is short and
direct. But why? Why should the church need to rely upon
forced exegesis to bring out the divine truths hidden away
in the obscurest passages of an ancient book? Such a view
of the hidden meaning of holy scripture was in part a consequence of the historical setting and conditioning of the
early Christian church, and, even earlier, as it had been during the ministry of Jesus and his apostles, when this was
taken for granted. The teacher was of necessity the ex-
pounder of a sacred book, and his advance upon its teaching
had perforce to be related to what was found there, as its
fulfillment or amplification or its true interpretation (see
Matt. 5.17-20, or almost any chapter of Paul or the Epistle
to Hebrews). By the same token, consistency required that
the meaning of the ancient scripture must agree with the
divine teaching of the new gospel.

This is the situation that lies behind the long and difficult struggle over scripture and tradition at successive church councils, not only Vatican II but Vatican I and even Trent. In fact, it is the nub of the argument between Catholicism and Protestantism, and so it has been for the past four centuries. It is still the problem confronting Protestant "ecumenism," not only in dealing with the reunion of the various reformed bodies, and with their divergent interpretations of scripture, but especially in dealing with the difficulty of relating Protestantism to both Orthodoxy and Anglicanism, with their stronger inheritance from the Catholic past. Surely one thing ought to be clear: the proliferation of dogmas based on scripture, and especially of those which have only a tenuous or inferential connection with scripture, ought to be discouraged. It is not necessary for a living church to possess five hundred pages of dogma. Nor is it necessary for every "pious opinion" to be settled, defined, and declared true or false, a dogma or a heresy. The basic doctrines of the Christian religion are few and simple—simple to state, profound to understand, difficult to realize, and hard to carry out or exemplify in daily living, indeed requiring divine grace for the achievement. Surely the *aggiornamento* or "up-dating" heralded by Pope John must include a simplification and a redefinition of the elemental teachings of the Christian faith, with a minimum of theological argumentation and amplification, and with a far more insistent emphasis upon their significance for human living, both personal and social. The philosophical and more abstruse theological implications and elaborations of dogma may be left to the experts, without binding these problems upon the weary shoulders of the ordinary Christian. This includes Protestant dogma quite as much as it does Roman Catholic and Orthodox.

Hitherto, the approach to church unity, or to Christian reunion, as it really should be called, has been very largely theological, even dogmatic. Elaborate studies of the basic teachings or tenets of the various religious bodies, Lutheran, Reformed, Orthodox, Anglican, Roman, and other, have been undertaken in the hope of finding a common denominator. But the progress made thus far in this direction has been disappointing. It has been useful, of course, as demonstrating wider areas of agreement than had been suspected. The churches are not so far apart, in many areas, as one might suppose. Indeed, the fundamental agreement of all Christians in their most basic beliefs and presuppositions, their faith in God, their unity in Christ, their acceptance of holy scripture, their search for norms as set forth in the apostolic age, their belief in divine inspiration and in the direct and positive guidance of the Holy Spirit, their hope for life to come, their stress upon the great virtues (chiefly love), their conception of sin, their experience of reconciliation and forgiveness, their dependence upon divine grace, their hope of future salvation—these and still other doctrines, teachings, or practices are common to all Christians everywhere.[9] The ratio between contested or rejected doctrines and those that are accepted and affirmed is probably very high: one to ten, or perhaps one to fifty, depending upon how highly we value the great central doctrines of our faith. There are, of course, a number of secondary doctrines, and even some that are tertiary—doctrines that depend upon other doctrines or upon varying interpretations of other doctrines.

But the initial obstacles to reunion are not mainly doctrinal: they are practical, historical, and psychological. Pope John XXIII wisely insisted that the Vatican Council should

9. See my *Basic Christian Beliefs*, Edinburgh and New York, 1960.

deal with these, rather than with dogmas. A new approach to the whole problem is required. A way must be hewn through the tangled jungle of prejudice that has blocked intercommunion and even communication between the different Christian groups for several long and dismal centuries. Furthermore, the practical, historical, psychological difficulties are themselves entangled with one another, and with dogmatic views and convictions. Above all there is the question of taking history and biblical research seriously. Often the biblical data and their interpretation greatly complicate the issue. Frequently the dogmatic grounds of disagreement are largely a rationalization of the historical—as may be seen, for example, in the division between East and West over the *filioque* clause in the Nicene Creed.[10] As the Earl of Balfour said in his Gifford Lectures, "Scratch a reason and find a cause."

Meanwhile, the demand for change, for reunion, for the knitting up of the torn and divided forces of the church is steadily growing. It is a tragedy of first magnitude that in a time when the moral strength of Christianity is challenged on all sides, when a constructive moral program and effort are called for as never before, the church is virtually impotent. The Christian religion does not bring a tenth of its potential force to bear upon the moral and social situation. In some places it is actually on the side of reaction and injustice—and not only in Viet Nam. The tocsin has sounded for a world-wide moral and spiritual awakening. God grant that the call may be heard and heeded, not only by Rome but by all the churches of Christ throughout the world and by all men of faith and good will everywhere!

10. See Cross, *Dictionary*, p. 504 ("Filioque"). See also p. 52 below.

II

The Beginning of the Papal Primacy: The Fifth Century

The average person has, probably, almost no conception of how great a part of the history of the Christian church is the history of the papacy—or, indeed, how great a part of the history of Europe and of Western civilization it is. On the whole, this has been a beneficent part, and in all probability neither the Christian church nor Western civilization could have survived without the papacy. The main outline of its history can be sketched briefly, in five or six broad panels.

The papacy emerged upon the fully lighted stage of world history in the fourth century, and it achieved its greatest initial advance in the two crucial centuries between Constantine and the end of the fifth century. The earlier history of the bishops of Rome, and of the Christian church as a whole, is more or less obscure and fragmentary—though we shall return to it. But once the persecutions were over, and the church was permitted to live an open and public life and to share in the events of political and social change, and when the need for a steadying power in the West became ever more and more insistent, the popes seized their opportunity—or rather, they saw their duty—and the world history of the papacy as an institution began. This crisis marked the real source and origin of the claim to primacy and world-wide authority. What had gone before was as nothing in comparison with the bold assertion of the right to universal dominion and decision and the supernatural authorization of both.

It used to be supposed in many quarters that all claims to empire were the work of wicked and conniving men, who planned thus to seize power and advantage for themselves. But the formula does not always work. It does not apply to ancient Rome, for example, whose expansion was drawn outward as by a vacuum; the condition of the times, especially in Asia Minor and the Near East, called for a firm, just, pacific, and pacifying hand in control of the destinies of whole nations. Nor does it explain the more recent expansion of Great Britain, in the East, in Asia, and in Africa: half the time the British went in by invitation. So likewise the papacy, as viewed from a purely historical, non-theological standpoint: its powers and responsibilities grew in response to obvious needs of the time. Order, security, peace, and the common welfare—these were the ends to safeguard which men put forth their best efforts, in reliance upon divine grace and with what seemed unquestionably the divine authorization. Scripture, tradition, and manifest destiny all combined to point the way. Such a man as Pope Leo I (440-61), who dominates the period that saw the rise of the papal power, was certainly no political adventurer!

The so-called triumph of the church under Constantine took place in a world in steady decline. After the golden age of the Antonines had ended, like an Indian summer followed by equinoctial tempests, the decline became swift and even sudden. The emperor Commodus (180-192) was no match for his father, the philosophic emperor Marcus Aurelius (161-80); and the mounting disasters and financial reverses of the empire, which now began, reached a climax under Decius (249-51). Beyond the borders, like hungry timber wolves, the barbarians waited to invade, ravage, and destroy. The persecutions of the Christians were in part motivated by these reverses and threats of further invasion. As Tertullian said, "If the Tiber rises to the walls, if the Nile fails to flood the fields, if the sky is motionless or the earth is not, if famine strikes, or plague, at once the cry is heard, 'The Christians to the lion!' " (*Apology* 40.2). As late as St. Augustine, the same cry was heard (*City of God* 2.3): the Vandals were everywhere, the City (Rome) had fallen, and the Christians were to blame!—for it was in consequence of their alien infiltration and their subversive influence that the gods had deserted the ancient temples on the Capitol and the Palatine.

The victory of Constantine and Licinius at the Milvian Bridge north of Rome (Oct. 28, 312) cut short the further continuation of Diocletian's persecution in the West.[1] In the East, Maximinus Daza died at Adrianople in April 313, when besieged by Licinius; so ended the persecution, and Christianity was recognized as a *religio licita*,[2] free to practice its cultus so far as this did not encourage anything *contra disciplinam*. But the church's victory was won at a price; the new champion of liberty, the patron of the church, turned out to be an exacting master. To this day men look back upon the victory as a questionable one, and there are Roman Catholics who would like to see the inheritance of the past completely rolled back "to the days

1. Bettenson, pp. 22f.
2. See the Appendix to my *Roman Hellenism and the New Testament,* New York and Edinburgh, 1962.

before Constantine." The consequences of the Constantinian triumph are still with the church, and the churches. For one thing, the church went too far, too fast, and from being a proscribed society which the Roman government had undertaken to exterminate, it was first tolerated, then embraced, then made the sole legal religion in the empire. Paganism was now proscribed, and a *Kulturkampf* followed, a war against civilization, in which (as under Theodosius I and later) the surviving art, literature, and philosophy of the ancient classical world were ruthlessly destroyed by the new barbarians. Worse yet, the survival (under modification) of the Hellenistic and Roman emperor cult affected all Christian relations with the state. The emperor undertook to settle the theological differences of the rival Christian sects and groups (or "heresies"), e.g. Arianism (in the fourth century) or the Donatist defection (311-411), either by conference or, as in the latter case, by main force.[3]

Thus the shift in outlook, in direction, in the center of gravity of the ancient world, was the result of no alteration or reversal—as in the fantastic "day the earth stood still." From now on, a persecuting empire, at last turned friendly and favorable, still continued to operate with all its ancient tools, its weapons and devices: the Christians were compelled to ride the tiger, or perish. There was certainly a mutual fusion of Christianity and antique culture; but, as we can now see clearly, pagan culture was then in decline, no longer the fresh, vigorous civilization of ancient Hellas. Thus a Christianized Roman Hellenism survived for many centuries: in the East as the Byzantine culture, in the West, eventually, as mediaeval Christianity. It is still potent, to this day. Much of lower-level Hellenistic religion survived and was taken over, following two periods of renaissance,

3. See Bettenson, pp. 31f.

by the church. Its darker aspects reached all the way from
gross superstition to the complete substitution of simple
"faith," i.e. credulity, for reason and scientific knowledge,
with an aversion for both science and philosophy, and a
total loss of the critical faculty, especially in historical
matters. It was not the western and northern barbarians
who destroyed Rome; Rome had been corrupt and on the
verge of collapse before they arrived on the scene. And the
task of the church was made infinitely harder as a result of
a long century and a half (161-313) of internal dry rot,
political irresponsibility, and inaction. That Western civilization survived, and that the church arrived in the nick of
time—arrived and asserted itself—is one of the miracles of
history. A generation or two more would have been too late.
By the date of the Islamic assault, all would have been over.

    It was a historical misfortune, nevertheless, that Con-
stantine and his sons and their successors were called upon
to settle the internal debates and quarrels of the church by
legal means, for the sake of peace and the welfare of the
empire. It was even more unfortunate that the church ever
engaged in these internal dissensions. But such was the historical situation, and there is no use in complaining about
what actually happened, or in deploring the unavoidable
circumstances and conditions that led to the scene. Arianism
might have been handled differently, had theologians been
less cantankerous and unyielding, and—perhaps—had it not
become the Christianity of the barbarous Goths. But Gnosticism, on the other hand, an earlier and more deeply rooted
perversion of Christian doctrine, could not have been tolerated if Christianity was to remain a historical religion and
not become a system of metaphysical speculation; for it was
a historical religion, its past grounded in the Greek translation of the ancient Hebrew scriptures, which the Gentile

church had used from its very beginning, and in the New Testament, their Christian supplement. Christianity was a religion that took history seriously, indeed in utter seriousness; and it simply could not compromise with the kaleidoscopic, phantasmagorian systems of speculation advanced by the Gnostic dreamers.

By 380, when Theodosius the Great (379-95) ruled the East and Gratian (375-83) the West, there was an end of all religious freedom.[4] Christianity was made the state religion and the Catholic Church the state church; heathenism was totally proscribed, and such theological variants as Arianism were stamped out with imperial support at the Council of Constantinople in 381. The rough and ready rule, in both East and West, required all "Romans" to accept the faith that the Apostle Peter had delivered to them, and that was now attested by Pope Damasus (366-84) and by his contemporary Peter II the bishop of Alexandria. This faith was centered in the sole godhead of Father, Son, and Holy Spirit, and was designed to outlaw paganism; but it also outlawed all Christian formulas that did not tally with the Nicene Creed—now revised into its present form as the "Niceno-Constantinopolitan" Creed, though it still commonly passes for the "Nicene."[5] The grief and anguish of heart which was caused devout pagans by this ancient act of uniformity is reflected in the story of the Altar of Victory in the Roman Senate, which the Christians removed, though it was a famous ancient symbol of loyalty and patriotism,[6] and in the ineffectual protest of Libanius against

4. Bettenson, pp. 30f.
5. Bettenson, pp. 34-7.
6. See Symmachus, *Third Relation*, translated in my *Ancient Roman Religion*, New York, 1957, pp. 246-51; see also my *Hellenistic Religions*, New York, 1953, pp. xvi and 149.

the wanton destruction of the treasures of classical art in the
East. The murder of Hypatia, a noble Neoplatonic philos-
opher, at Alexandria in 415 by a mob of illiterate Nitrian
monks was an example of the stupid fanaticism unleashed
by the imperial champions of orthodoxy—the mob had been
incited by the Archbishop Cyril. The *odium theologicum*—
theological animosity—is bad enough; but when combined
with and supported by political compulsion or encouragement, acting in the interest of religious uniformity, the
result is—for the church—treason and betrayal of the very
spirit of the gospel.

But imperial intervention was inevitable, in view of the
low level of intelligence and learning in the decadent fourth
and fifth centuries, and in view of the strange caricatures
of Christianity that posed as the "true" teaching, not to say
the one and only orthodox formulation and interpretation
of church doctrine! At the same time the stiffer organization of the church, its concern with legal enactments
(canons), its more rigid rules governing admission to membership, its more detailed discipline, its elaboration of public
worship, its enlarged calendar, and the growth of monasti-
cism with a strict, all-embracing rule of life, its far-flung
missionary advance in the East and North, its various Bible
translations, even its developing art and architecture—all this
showed the organized *militia Christi*, the "legionaries of the
cross," to be "alive and on the march" in a darkening world.
And it was not a day too soon! Nothing could more strongly
have encouraged the developing tendency of the time toward a centralized authority than the church's apparent
growth and success under the new auspices of the Roman
government.

As church historians insist, the end of the fourth century
and the beginning of the fifth marked the high point in the

story of the ancient Catholic church. It had never before been so favorably situated, vis-à-vis the empire and the world at large. It was now the recognized state religion, and the majority of human beings within the empire were at least subject to the church, if not all of them actually members. The emperors not only protected the church from heresy and schism but fostered its missionary advances, its legislation, and its church building. It was the era of the classical patristic theology, championed by Augustine and Jerome in the West and by Chrysostom, Cyril, Theodoret, and the Cappadocians in the East.

But it was the balmy hour before the hurricane! Theodosius the Great died in 395, and this was a signal for the beginning of the long awaited disruption between East and West, which were henceforth increasingly to go their separate, widely divergent ways. Although Byzantium, "New Rome," continued to maintain the fiction of the Roman Empire for another thousand years, the invasion of the Germanic tribes in the West put an end almost at once to the legend of *Roma aeterna*. The barbarians, especially the Goths or Germans, many of them converted to Arianism by Ulfilas, had their own bishops, rites, and Bible. But the tide did not turn in an instant. The barbarian invasion is not to be envisioned as a human flood sweeping across the boundaries of the empire; instead, it was at first the intrusion, here and there, of groups who settled within the imperial territory and slowly infiltrated its society. Only after this slow "softening up" and on occasions of great pressure or inducement were there real old-style invasions like those of the ancient Celts, as when Alaric the Goth sacked Rome in 410 and Attila the Hun advanced upon it in 452. The Roman retreat was marked by the abandonment of Aquileia, the creation of the temporary see of Grado, the rebuilding

of Ravenna, the final stand at Torcello. By the year 500 the
Roman rule in the West was a thing of the past.

But in the midst of this raging universal storm and
tempest, the West deserted by the imperial authorities, its
rulers weak and inept, the Catholic Church stood firm.
Many of its people were now subject to the German invaders, especially in the North; many, in the villages, were
swept away by the surviving heathen—e.g. at Subiaco, where
St. Benedict had begun his missionary work. Tidal waves
of barbarians now overwhelmed the West, until only Italy
(and not all of Italy) and part of Gaul remained to the
empire. Driven by the Huns in their rear, the East and West
Germans moved westward and southward. The West Goths
entered Spain; the Vandals followed, and moved on to
North Africa in 429; the Burgundians had already established a kingdom on the Rhine in 413; the East Goths
entered Italy in 488.

In the very middle of this discouraging century arose
a figure destined to influence the whole later history of
Europe and the world. This was Pope Leo I, "the Great"
(440-61), who refused to bow to circumstance and forced
events to follow him. His influence even reached the East,
as when he sent his famous letter or "Tome" to the Council
of Chalcedon (451),[7] cutting a practical and intelligible
passage through the tangled mazes of theological controversy, and winning approval for his simple yet profound
solution of the problems of Christology. His most dramatic
and heroic hour was when he faced the wild barbarians
under Attila, in 452—see Raphael's famous painting in the
Vatican Gallery, or Alessandro Algardi's great relief in
St. Peter's. He repeated the event in 455 when he bade the
Vandal Geiserich begone. Although his status was only that

7. Bettenson, pp. 69-72; Denzinger, §§ 290-95.

of metropolitan and patriarch, on a par with the heads of the church in Constantinople and Alexandria, his influence soon far exceeded theirs. The former was little more than chaplain to the Eastern emperor; the latter lost most of his influence by overbidding his hand at Chalcedon—his defeat was followed by the endless internecine struggles with the Monophysites, who thenceforth dominated Syria and Egypt.

It was Pope Leo I who did more than any other man in history to lay the secure foundations of the Roman papacy. He was the first to become the real "Bishop of the West," or "Bishop of the bishops in the West." He practically took the place of the Roman emperor in Italy, a land now forsaken and left vacant, to the peril of every area west and north of the Adriatic. He first set forth clearly the principle of the papal primacy, appealing, with the exegesis of his own day, to the traditional texts: Matt. 16.18, "Thou art Peter"; Luke 22.32, "Strengthen thy brethren"; John 21.15-17, "Feed my sheep." [8] Assuming that these passages referred to Peter's successors as well as to the Apostle himself, they affirmed the authorization by the divine Head of the church of the claims now made for the bishop of Rome, who was accordingly given the title "Vicar of Christ." Ignoring 2 Corinthians 11.28, where Paul refers to *his* responsibility and anxiety for "all the churches," the duty of caring for them was now understood to belong to Peter. This theory, basically political and practical in its origin and presuppositions, opened a way that led far across the coming centuries, all the way to 1870 and the decree of Papal Infallibility, and beyond.

It was an uncritical age. Not only could texts of scripture be wrested to yield whatever meaning the interpreter preferred, but the partisans of particular views did not hesi-

8. Mirbt, §§ 169f.

tate to revise the earlier documents that covered their case. Canon VI of the Council of Nicaea was altered to read: "The primacy has always belonged to the Church of Rome" —*Ecclesia romana semper habuit primatum.*[9] But this was only a falling back upon an imperial decree of 445, in which Valentinian III drew up the short and simple rule: "From now on the peace of the churches will everywhere be served if they all recognize it [i.e. the church of Rome] as the ruler"—*Tunc enim demum ecclesiarum pax ubique servabitur si rectorem suum agnoscat universitas.* Leo was not wholly fortunate in his successors, though on the whole his outspoken insistence upon the Roman pontiff's right to rule was generally acknowledged and repeated. Felix III (483-92) promptly excommunicated the "Diophysite" ("Two natures") patriarch, Acacius of Constantinople, for his compromise with Zeno, and so completed the breach between East and West. His successor Gelasius I (492-6) notified the emperor Anastasius I that he was himself, as a priest and a dispenser of the sacraments, superior to any earthly ruler—he was even responsible for the spiritual welfare of the emperor.[10] (The so-called *Decree of Gelasius,* which lists the canonical books of the Bible, is a private writing of some sixth-century scholar; parts of it, however, go back to the fourth century, i.e. to Pope Damasus, 366-84.[11]) Pope Symmachus (498-514) went still further, and insisted that the pope could be judged by no man;[12] he also began (513) the custom of awarding the pallium (a woolen scarf) to bishops and archbishops.

9. Mirbt, § 111.

10. Denzinger, § 347. See the note (XI) in James Bryce, *The Holy Roman Empire,* New York, 1961, p. 453.

11. Denzinger, §§ 350-54; Mirbt, § 191; see Heussi's note, p. 131.

12. Denzinger, § 362.

After the year 500 came a full spate of forgeries in favor of the papal primacy or supremacy: false acts of martyrs, false decrees of synods, all leading up to the fictitious legend of St. Sylvester (314-35) and the "forged decretals," chiefly *The Donation of Constantine*.[13] According to the latter, Constantine had been a persecutor of the church and was therefore punished with leprosy. But in Rome he was converted by the good Pope Sylvester, healed, restored to health, and then baptized. In return he conferred upon the pope the title to all church rights, privileges, and properties, the unoccupied imperial Lateran Palace (the first basilica in Rome), together with the diadem, purple robes, scepter, royal title, and the right to maintain a court (*curia*) equal in rank to that of the emperor. The gift also included the city of Rome and the whole of Italy, the western provinces, their fortifications and their cities. In other words, this late (eighth century) document, the climax of the legend, authorized and supported the papal claim to a complete take-over of the Western empire, or what was left of it. For hundreds of years this forgery was accepted without question. The humanist Laurentius Valla first proved it unauthentic, but his book was not published until 1519, twenty-five years after his death. The basic idea underlying the false decretal certainly goes back to the late fifth century, when almost any device seemed justified if only peace and order could thereby be restored in a world that was gradually reverting to chaos.

Looking backward, we can now make out some of the factors that led, historically, to the papal supremacy. According to the historian Karl Heussi, "It was no inheritance from the early days of Christianity or from the gospel, but the creation of the ancient Roman spirit in the field of

13. Bettenson, pp. 135-40; Mirbt, § 228. See also pp. 73f below.

Catholic ecclesiasticism." [14] Less impartial historians have
referred to "the ghost of the Caesars"—but that is often
only sarcasm, and ignores the great positive values represented by, in fact created by, the Roman papacy, not only
in the fourth and fifth centuries but during the many more
centuries that followed. It is still one of the most valuable
social and religious assets that the Christian church and the
Western world possess. The earliest origins of the papal
supremacy of course go back to the period before Constantine, when the organization of the church under metropolitans and patriarchs began (approved by Canons IV
and V of Nicaea).[15] The patriarchates or primatial sees of
Rome, Alexandria, Antioch, Carthage, Caesarea (in Cappadocia), Heraclea, and Ephesus, likewise Constantinople,
when formed, included vast areas of adjacent territory. The
process of organization was virtually completed during the
seventy years between the councils of Constantinople (381)
and Chalcedon (451). In this development, Rome obviously occupied the widest and fairest field, met the sternest
urgency, and faced the direst need. For a time the process
had been retarded, at least in the West, by the exigencies
of Byzantine church policy and Eastern church law. But
by the fifth century these deterrents had weakened, and
the convergence of positive forces was such that the papal
primacy became inevitable and indisputable.

The papal primacy meant a break with the past, even in
the West, where Cyprian's theory (ca. 250) of a collegial
episcopate exercising oligarchical rule over the church had
hitherto been dominant: [16] it was the theory known to this
day as "episcopalism," as contrasted with both papalism and

14. Heussi, p. 128.
15. Mirbt, §§ 109f.
16. Bettenson, pp. 101-4; Mirbt, §§ 66f.

"curialism" (rule by the pope or the papal court). That the new theory, viz. the papal primacy or "supremacy," cannot have been widely held before or during the time of Constantine is clear from such an obvious fact as the failure of that emperor to deal with the pope as the representative authority in the West, even in matters closely relating to the unity of the church. For example, during the early days of the Donatist schism, in convoking the Council of Arles (314), at which for the first time all bishops of the western provinces of the empire were bidden to assemble, no suggestion was made that the Bishop of Rome should issue the call. Again, Eusebius, in his *History of the Church* (ca. 324), nowhere suggests that the Roman bishop enjoyed pre-eminence over all his episcopal colleagues elsewhere. And the famous sixth Canon of Nicaea (325), in its original form, mentions only the patriarchal dignity of Rome, Alexandria, and Antioch, not the papal. The very absence of a particular reference to Rome was doubtless the temptation that led to later tampering with the text—as we have already seen.

From a purely objective, historical point of view, it is clear that one of the chief factors in the rise of the papal supremacy, in the West, was the removal of the emperor and his administration to "New Rome," the new capital on the Bosporus. This was unquestionably a retreat from an increasingly difficult situation, by an emperor blind to the rising dangers in the East, dangers that were destined eventually to prove fatal. Into the political vacuum in the West moved the only strong, effective force capable of insuring law and order—as Pope Leo proved it to be.

Moreover, efficiency—or effectiveness—demanded an executive authority centered in one person who could speak and act for the church when occasion required, without the delays and divisions of a large deliberative and legislative assembly of bishops. Clearly this was the meaning of the rise of metropolitical groups and patriarchates; but in the West there was only one, and in the East, after Chalcedon, there was only one that really counted. From then onward, the "Ecumenical Patriarch" of Constantinople, the recognized head of the church in the East, was matched and balanced by the pope in the West, thus creating a rivalry in which the Eastern head was often outmaneuvered and left in the rear. To begin with, he was greatly handicapped by too close a proximity and too constant an association with the imperial court. Furthermore, the problems of the East, the endless hair-splitting theological wrangles, and the mounting political pressure from north, east, and south, culminating in the Arab conquests in the seventh century, left little time or opportunity for the discussion or even the contemplation of world-history in the making, such as men faced every day in the West. As contrasted with the compliant Eastern patriarchs, the spirit of the Western bishops, especially the bishop of Rome, was a heroic love of freedom, deep concern for the church and for the people of Italy, and a determination to maintain their liberty against all comers.

Furthermore, the downfall of the western half of the empire and the encroachment of the barbarians encouraged in Rome itself a stronger national spirit than had existed since the days of the old Roman Republic, and it led to a concentration of loyalty upon the only surviving national institution, the Christian church, and its head, the first citizen of Rome. The services of the popes in the preservation of Hellenistic-Roman culture and civilization, learning and art (contrast the ferocious destructive violence of such Eastern monarchs as Theodosius I and Justinian)—this alone would have earned them the affectionate gratitude and loyalty of all intelligent men and women everywhere in the West.

Still another factor in the situation was the papal championship of orthodoxy, especially Pope Leo's intervention at the ecumenical Council of Chalcedon, where, though not present in person but by representatives, his voice was heard and his advice was taken.[17] Rome did not favor "endless genealogies" of ideas, the subtle spinning out of speculations until one could scarcely recall where the theory began; Rome favored a brief, practical, comprehensible, authoritative statement that summed up the gist of the matter and presented the alternatives with daylight clarity. Thus even in the second century, in dealing with Gnosticism, the practical solution, viz. the appeal to the Apostolic writings, the Apostolic creed, and the Apostolic traditions of the great sees, had been the solution adopted, first at Rome and then by the whole church. At its center was the Apostolic creed, fundamentally the old Roman baptismal creed,[18] of which traces can be found in the middle of that century. On such minor problems as the Paschal controversy and heretical baptism, and on such major ones as the support of the Logos Christology and eventually the Nicene definition, where Rome was consistently on the side of orthodoxy and strongly supported Athanasius—so much so that one could almost say that orthodoxy *was* what Rome supported!— in all these crises the Roman church was clearly in the right, as judged by the later church, and "on the side of the angels." There was no ignoring the actual services of the Roman church to the cause of Christ. No wonder if men rewarded them with their further confidence and loyalty!

17. Bettenson, pp. 69-72.
18. Bettenson, pp. 33f. Cross, pp. 72f. ("Apostles' Creed").

To crown all there was the steadily increasing veneration
of St. Peter. It began with Pope Damasus, or even earlier,
when the saint's burial place was honored, and special devo-
tions were attached thereto, and when the Bishop of Rome
began to refer to his own as the "apostolic" (not "patriarchal") see. For example, the ancient statue of the Apostle
that now adorns the Basilica of St. Peter on the epistle side
of the nave, near the high altar, dates from the fifth century,
and may well have been placed in the earlier Constantinian
Basilica by Pope Leo himself—it was originally in St. John
Lateran.

Thus it was that even prior to Pope Leo the way had been
cleared and prepared for the explicit announcement of the
papal primacy. Already in the fourth century Rome was a
decisive factor in the church's development of doctrine, discipline, and worship, in Christian education and the incul-
cation of Christian morals. The early councils (the four
recognized by Anglicans and most Protestants and even the
seven recognized by the Eastern churches) knew nothing of
any absolute standing or authority of the Roman pontiff.
The Pope's legates were welcomed and heard, but they did
not preside. Nevertheless, the great leaders in the Roman line
of succession, men like Julius I (337-52), Damasus I (366-
84), Siricius (384-99), Innocent I (402-17), worked steadily
in the direction of greater authority, and thus prepared the
way for Leo (440-61). But "the time was not yet" when all
the theological and practical corollaries of this leadership
were to be declared. Even the great St. Augustine (354-
430) failed to recognize the pope as the church's infallible
teacher of the faith. His references to the pope do not imply
that the pope was a pre-eminent figure in the religious life
of Christians, let alone the decisive figure in dogmatic pro-
nouncements. When Rome agreed with Augustine, he de-

clared the question closed. (See his *Sermon 131*, ch. 10.)
The famous saying, *Roma locuta, causa finita est*, "Rome
has spoken; the case is closed," does not go back to him in
quite this form, but very nearly: *Causa finita est*, "The
case is closed; *would* that the error [of Pelagianism] might
also be ended!—*utinam aliquando finiatur error*." [19] But on
the other hand, he held that a council might correct a
Roman pronouncement, if it was mistaken (and disagreed
with the saint?)—see *Epistle 43*, 7(19). His views were still
essentially the North African, which he had inherited from
Tertullian and Cyprian. The epistle, dated 397, was addressed to a group of friends, and others whom it might
concern, and it dealt with an appeal against an unsatisfactory
decision in Rome. "Suppose those bishops who decided the
case at Rome were *not* good judges: there still remained a
plenary council of the whole universal church, where these
judges themselves might be put on the defensive, and where,
if convicted of being mistaken, their decision might be
reversed"—*restabat adhuc plenarium ecclesiae universae con-
cilium, ubi etiam cum ipsis judicibus causa posset agitari,
ut [et?], si male judicasse convicti essent, eorum sententiae
solverentur.*

A recent historical novel, *Gregory the Great*, by a
pseudonymous Austrian author, "Gerhart Ellert," maintains that upon the ruins of the Roman Empire Pope Gregory laid the foundations of the Christian West. Gregory's
service to civilization was indispensable, but I believe the
process really began with Pope Leo, a century and more
earlier. And, I regret to add, the unknown author assumes
that the sixth-century papacy had existed from the first
century—there had been no development. The title of address, "Holy Father," was age-old, according to the author,

19. Mirbt, § 157.

yet it was also—and still is—the title of the Eastern patriachs, especially of the "ecumenical" patriach in Constantinople. He also assumes that the Arians, who did not recognize Christ's deity, were "worse than pagans" (p. 7). This is all propaganda, not history, and even a historical novel should be more accurate and objective.

III

The "Dark" Ages: 500-900

The year 500 marked the all but audible tick of that cosmic clock for which "one day is as a thousand years, and a thousand years as one day" (2 Peter 3.8). It was a muffled tick, and then the great pendulum slowly reversed itself and started its long swing in the opposite direction. For in that year, A.D. 500, or at most only a short time earlier, Clovis, king of the Salian Franks, having defeated the Romans of northern Gaul at the Battle of Soissons in 486, decided to become a Christian. He was baptized by St. Remigius at Rheims on Christmas Day, and with him three thousand of his subjects. *Mitis depone colla, Sigamber,* said the godly bishop; *adora quod incendisti; incende quod adorasti!* "Gently bow the neck, noble Sigambrian; adore what you have burned; burn what you have adored!" [1] This hour marked one of the turning points in church history, even in world history; for, as the East steadily retreated in upon itself, the West was faced with a widening door of opportunity, the like of which had never before been seen. The church's task in the early Roman Empire had

1. Migne, *Patrologia Latina*, LXXI, col. 227.

49

been foredoomed to a merely partial success; the entrenched
paganism of the long past was too massive, inert, immobile,
and its civilization was already moribund. But the fresh
northern peoples, just emerging from barbarism, offered a
far more promising field for evangelism, education, and
molding in the ways of the gospel; and so it surely must
have appeared to the bishops of Gaul who accompanied
and assisted Remigius. And so it proved. Just at the strategic
moment—at the precise tick of the cosmic timepiece—a new
direction was taken in historical development. "Man's ex-
tremity is God's opportunity." This thing has happened
more than once in human history. The discovery of America and the consequent shift from East to West, once more,
at the end of the fifteenth century, is another striking example. As Pope Leo in the fifth century had seized the
"main chance" and turned with the tide, so now another
turning was made, and the heroic figures who dominated
the four dark centuries that followed included such men
as Pope Gregory the Great, St. Benedict, and Charlemagne.

The contrast between the new age and all that had gone
before in church history is clear and striking. Before 500,
the church's center of gravity had been located in the East,
with its larger Christian population, its spiritual and theological interests, its widespread controversies, its councils,
and its settlement of dogmatic discords; and from Constantine onward the East crowned all this by including the new
capital of the empire, Byzantium, "New Rome." But from
500 to 800, the date of Charlemagne's coronation as head
of the "Holy" Roman Empire, which now rivaled and sup-
planted the old Roman Empire in the East, it was evident
that the West was steadily becoming the more progressive,
crucial, creative half of the Christian world. The West had

now entered upon its long career of expansion, which, though with more than one serious setback, has continued ever since. The fall of the Western empire; the conversion of the Franks; the establishment of the new "Holy" Roman Empire to take the place of the old (albeit in theory continuous with it)—all this was as clean a shift as those in earlier history when world power passed from the old oriental empires of Babylon, Nineveh, and Egypt, first to Persia, then to the new Macedonian empire, finally to Rome.

Involved from the very first in this shift in the center of gravity from East to West were the tiny cracks that grew eventually into open rifts and schisms, including the "Great Schism" between the Eastern and Western churches, which continues to this day. As early as 484-519 there had been a thirty-five-year breach after Pope Felix III banned the Patriarch Acacius of Constantinople—who had gone back on the decisions reached at Chalcedon. But worse dissensions were to come, all the way to the great division of 1054. Yet it must not be thought that these frictions were only accidental. Like earthquakes, landslides, open ruptures in the earth, they were the result of long-existing faults or tensions lying deep out of sight and far below the surface. The basic antagonisms were very old.

The real grounds of separation between East and West go back to the early centuries, and they were partly psychological, partly political, partly ethnic and even linguistic. In fact, there had been obvious tension between East and West long before the rise of Christianity. The steady advance of Roman power across the Balkan peninsula, then across Asia Minor, then sweeping into Egypt and the Near East; the threat of Antony and Cleopatra to divide the new republican empire and rule the East from Egypt; the plot

of Avidius Cassius and Faustina the Younger to achieve the
same goal of independence, now with Antioch the capital;
the shift of ancient Rome to "New" Rome by Constantine;
the restless peace maintained by force along the frontiers,
including those of the East, until the slow collapse was
completed and first the barbarians and then the Arabs swept
over the eastern Mediterranean world; the unwelcome administration of Italy by the Eastern empire; finally the
Crusades and the plundering of the East by barbarous
"Romans" from the West—all this long discouraging tale
of East-West relations belongs to the background of the
tensions between Byzantium and Rome in the ecclesiastical
sphere. It is ridiculous to ignore it, and its causes, and
confine the story to the theological debates of church
councils and their dogmatic decrees. The debates and the
decrees were heavily tinged, not to say sometimes actually
occasioned, by the political and social tensions of the time,
accumulated as a vast burden of prejudice and ill will from
the long unhappy past.

Such an ostensible ground of separation as the famous
filioque clause in the "Nicene" Creed contained unsuspected
dynamite. To say with the East that the Holy Spirit "proceeds from the Father *through* the Son" had ample scrip-
tural authority. But so also had the Western alternative,
"from the Father *and* the Son." Why then the quarrel?
The phrases—not now a diphthong, as had been the difference between the famous *homoousios* ("of one substance")
and *homoiousios* ("of like substance") during the Arian
period—were not even full phrases, in the original, but concerned a Greek preposition (*dia*, "through") and a Latin
enclitic (*que*, "and"). But look deeper. The phrase "through
the Son," if one imagined it symbolically, *could* be taken in

the sense of the abhorred Gnostic chain of aeons, one above
another, as in the accompanying diagram.

This conception was clearly false to the Christian teaching
as a whole and specifically to the New Testament as a
whole. But envisioned in a horizontal series,

one gets only an impression of the early but now antiquated
Modalism, or Sabellianism, or Dynamistic Monarchianism—
doctrines that emphasized the mode of revelation of the
godhead but sacrificed the distinction between the divine
persons—or some view even more remote from the central
theological tradition of the church. Hence there emerged
the symbol familiar to centuries of Christian art and architecture, the triangle—which should, however, be inverted,
or rotated 60° to the right, as the Spirit proceeds from both
the Father and the Son. Out of such simple elements grow

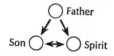

theological differences, and from them great dissensions
result—not from profound exercises in logic but from defects in human imagination, and over-literalism in human
thought, and the spirit of pugnacity and will-to-dominate,
and the lust to compel the faith of other men. The "defense

of the true faith" is often represented as a heroic and noble thing, inspired by courage and self-sacrifice; but alas, much of the tale is merely sordid and disgraceful and adds nothing to the luster of the Christian way of life.

The three centuries from 500 to 800 were indeed a dark age, and men could be forgiven for "looking after those things that were coming on the earth." In such ages, whose economic and political handicaps are little realized though their consequences are widely felt—in such an age, and even from an earlier beginning, say around 250, the tensions between peoples and groups were exacerbated, and molehills of friction grew into mountains of resentment.

In the year 416, Rutilius Claudius Namatianus, a late Latin poet, indeed the last of them, wrote his *Voyage Home to Gaul*.[2] In it he bade farewell to Rome, where he, a pagan, had held high office under a Christian government, and returned disheartened to his native town, probably somewhere near Toulouse. Here he was to face barbarian depredations even more severe than those already suffered in the South. It was only six years after the first "fall" of Rome in eight hundred years. The Goths under Alaric had captured and sacked the city in 410; and in 455 Genseric and his Vandals were to raid it again. The traditional date of the "fall" of Rome is 476, but this is merely the date of the downfall of the last Western emperor, the insignificant Romulus Augustulus, deposed by the German Odoacer. There was no sudden break in relations with the East. Theodoric (454-526), king of the Ostrogoths, a pro-Roman if ever there was one among the barbarians, undertook to establish an Italian state which should carry on the great tradition of Rome, its culture and civilization. But he died in 526, and Justinian slowly and with great effort recon-

2. See Loeb Classical Library: *Minor Latin Poets*, 1934, pp. 764ff.

quered Italy. From 535 to 555 Belisarius and Narses waged intermittent wars against the Goths, with terrible slaughter and ruin throughout Italy. In the latter year, the city, ruined and exhausted by these twenty years of devastation, was captured by the Eastern emperor, and for the next two centuries, until 751, Italy was administered by an imperial appointee, the exarch of Ravenna. But this official was no bulwark of security. Five times the city of Rome was captured, sacked, and recaptured during the Gothic Wars, and repeatedly threatened by the Lombards, the *Longobardi*. Her network of eleven ancient aqueducts was broken, and the water supply ceased—except for a few wells and the tawny, open Tiber. "For twenty-seven years," wrote Pope Gregory, "we lived in terror of the Lombards, nor can I say how much we had to pay them. There is an imperial treasurer with the army at Ravenna; but here I am the treasurer. Likewise, I have to provide for the clergy, the poor, and the people, and even to aid other churches in distress." [3]

During these troubled centuries the bishops of Rome took over more and more of the civil administration, as the officers of the now distant government lost their influence or failed to be reappointed. Thanks to the initiative and energy of Pope Gregory the Great (590-604) Rome recovered from the disasters of the Gothic wars. The Byzantine government, too remote and too involved in its own affairs, was inclined to overlook the needs of the West; as a consequence, it proved more and more incapable of maintaining law and order beyond the Adriatic. Eventually, Pope Leo III (795-816) chose Charlemagne, the strongest of the ortho-

3. *Epistle 5*, § 21, to the Empress Constantina. On Pope Gregory and the Lombards, see F. Holmes Dudden, *Gregory the Great*, 1905, I, 80-98; II, 3-42.

dox Frankish rulers, and crowned him emperor on Christmas Day in the year 800. Thus the "Holy" Roman Empire
was founded, independent of the East, and in fact its inevitable rival. It was the only power that could, under the
circumstances, maintain order and continue the tradition
of Roman authority in the West. But out of this change
grew the later bitter rivalry between the Popes and the
German Hohenstaufen, and the claims to sovereignty on
the part of the French and the Hapsburg rulers, and their
consequent interference in the affairs of Italy, including
those of the papacy.

Thus the rift between East and West long antedated the
crucial division in 1054. And thus the foundation of the
temporal power of the popes was laid in a great social crisis,
during which they rescued civilization from the threat of
total barbarism. And thus the emergence of the northern
barbarians and their rise to power and influence, and the
further progress of their cultural development, likewise
stemmed from this alliance between the papacy and the
northern sovereigns. And thus, finally, the split between
South and North, destined to lead eventually to the Reformation and the Counter Reformation, to Gallicanism
and Ultramontanism, and to centuries of occupation by
foreign armies—all this stemmed from the chaotic conditions that prevailed from the fifth century to the ninth.

Across the weakened borders of the empire first swept
the East German tribes, who were largely Arian; their
arrival caused a temporary flurry, but soon they were either
destroyed or romanized and absorbed into the settled Catholic population—e.g. in northern Italy, as around Milan and
Ravenna. This invasion was only an episode. The great and
permanently significant event was the conversion of the
West Germans, which began with Clovis and his Franks

in 500. Here was a population that could not be absorbed, could certainly not be destroyed, and was already in process of romanization by their own absorption of the culture and religion of the Romano-Gallic peoples whom they had invaded. A long process of mutual infiltration thus began and continued, with repeated reverses, for many centuries, until eventually it triumphed in the thoroughly Catholicized France of the Middle Ages. So powerful was this new group of northern peoples that missionary—and also military—efforts were successful against the heathen still farther to the north.

Thus the Catholic Church in the West began its world-historical task of subduing, pacifying, Christianizing, and educating the barbarians beyond the frontiers of the empire. *Lampadas echontes paradōsousin allois*—"Having torches they pass them on to others"—this is the good rule that has guided all civilized peoples from time immemorial (cf. Plato, *Laws* 6.776b). Only, in this case, the culture was deeply religious, and its motivation was something more than the promotion of the values of general education and welfare, trade and prosperity. The monastic orders, chiefly the Benedictines, were the torchbearers, the teachers, the guides and instructors of the nations, in agriculture, book-keeping, cattle-breeding, weaving and other domestic arts, as well as in reading, writing, and arithmetic, the copying of books, the collection of libraries, the treasuring of art and learning. What later Europe and all the world owes to these pioneers is incalculable. Behind the movement was the inspiration of the papacy, chiefly of Gregory the Great, not a great theologian though an influential one, but a great leader, planner, propagandist for missions, an aristocrat and statesman who at his own expense built six monasteries in Sicily and one in Rome. He did much to raise the standards of the clergy (see his *Regula Pastoralis*); he approved and promoted the work of St. Benedict, whose monastery at Monte Cassino had been destroyed by the Lombards in 585; and in 597 he sent Augustine on his mission to the Angli in Britain. And it was Gregory the Great, at the end of the sixth century, who was the real founder of the secular (or "temporal") power of the papacy in Italy. This rested chiefly upon the steady increase of territory acquired by the Roman church (i.e. the diocese of Rome; see any good map), especially the vast latifundia (*patrimonia*) received by gift or inheritance in central and southern Italy. These estates grew in time into the Papal States, separately governed and administered, sometimes well, often ill, until reclaimed by the Italian government in 1870.

Gregory acknowledged the authority of the Byzantine (now the "Eastern") emperor in Italy; nevertheless, it was Gregory himself who ruled the country and in the eyes of the populace was their sovereign, not the feeble exarch of Ravenna who represented the Eastern emperor during the two centuries from 555 to 751. In 593 he bought off the invading Lombards at the gates of Rome, and also overcame the pest by the help of St. Michael—hence Hadrian's tomb, now surmounted by this archangelic figure, became the Castel Sant' Angelo; in 599 he mediated the peace between the now-settled Lombards and the Byzantine court. Above all, Gregory was the first pope to realize fully the importance of the northern tribes, and to seek to ally them firmly with the papal throne. Even in Spain, his relations with the West Goths (Visigoths) betokened an enduring and historically significant relation. This was not an extension of jurisdiction but an expansion of influence. Two great barbarian women had much to do with it: Brunhilde, Queen of the Franks, and Theodelinde, Queen of the Lombards.

In converting the West Goths in Spain to Catholic Christianity at the Council of Toledo in 589, the phrase *filioque* was used in the creed to signify their renunciation of Arianism. But where jurisdiction was feasible, and the claim could be made good, it was imposed: as among the Angles in Britain, who were persuaded to accept the Roman calendar and customs, organization and supremacy. Even though Gregory's successors were notably lacking in his energy, skill, tact, foresight, and long-range planning, the papacy never receded in principle—or at least never in theory—from the high claims he had made in the name of religion and civilization, of Christ and the Church, and St. Peter.

In his relations with the East, Gregory, who once had been a kind of papal nuncio (*apokrisiarios*) in Constantinople, was unhesitating and firm. When the ecumenical patriarch, John IV the Faster, undertook to administer corporal punishment to two of his monks who were charged with heresy, Gregory intervened, condemned the patriarch as proud and irreverent, and declared the monks to be orthodox. He also rebuked the Byzantine patriarch for claiming the pretentious title of "ecumenical," and stressed his own, the noblest ever claimed by the papacy and used to this day: *servus servorum Dei*, "servant of the servants of God."

The condition of the Eastern church in this period was one of steady decline. Following the brilliant reign of Justinian I (527-65), the process of retrenchment and hemming-in of the receding Eastern empire became ever more inexorable. Visigoths, Lombards, Avars, Slavs, Bulgars, even the Persians on the far eastern borders held the Byzantine power in a vice-like grip. Despite the spectacular efforts of Heraclius (610-41) to repel the Persians, and his recovery of the True Cross at Ctesiphon in 629, the empire

was hopelessly divided by warring sects and parties. Again
Rome intervened, in the interest of orthodoxy, peace, and
good sense. At the Sixth Ecumenical Council, held at Constantinople in 680—known as the *Trullanum*, since it was
held in "Trullus," a domed hall in the royal palace—a letter
from Pope Agatho was received in which Monothelitism
(the view that Christ had a single "will") was roundly condemned. It also condemned the views of Pope Honorius
(625-38), whose curious lapse from orthodoxy set a severe
problem for the infallibilists at Vatican Council I in 1870.
A second "Trullan" Council was held in 692—often called
the *Quinisext*, as it supplemented both the Fifth and Sixth
General Councils.[4] At this Council a series of rules were
adopted, including recognition of all eighty-five, instead of
the fifty "Apostolic" canons recognized in the West; it rejected the rule of celibacy for presbyters and deacons; it
forbade the sabbatical fast on Sundays in Lent or on Satur-
days (except in Holy Week); it affirmed the binding authority of Acts 15.29 (the four rules laid down by the
Apostles in Jerusalem, prohibiting food offered to idols,
blood, i.e. non-kosher meat, meat of animals strangled
(*terefa*), and fornication); and it forbade—as idolatry—the
popular Western representation of Christ as the Lamb of
God.

One can only view this period in Byzantine church
history with sadness and regret. From our modern vantage
point, nothing could have been more tragic than the blind
complacency and indifference with which the East failed
to prepare to meet the advancing world crisis, the Muslim
terror of the seventh century. Of course Monophysitism
(the doctrine of one nature in Christ) was a debatable view,
and so was Monothelitism (one will in Christ), which fol-

4. Mirbt, § 224. Cross, pp. 1378f. ("Trullan Synod").

lowed it. They seemed to make Christ only a deity in
disguise, as if it were the old docetic Gnosticism all over
again—in truth the apparition of a pagan god, not really
either God or man, but a third kind of being, neither "perfectly man" nor "truly God," as the Council of Chalcedon
had required. Both theories, with their attendant speculations, deserved to be discouraged. They assumed a knowledge of the nature of Christ and an understanding of the
terms being used which no one has ever possessed; and in
the end they probably tried to say more or less what orthodoxy was saying, only in different language—certainly
Nestorius was trying to say it. But from the practical or
the historical point of view, what could have been more
futile and tragic, as a preparation for coming events on the
stage of world history? It was as if some stately ship, under
a lowering sky and with a falling glass, were moving steadily
on toward an unseen horizon, where sea and sky were indis-
tinguishable—*ponto nox incubat atro!*—while its officers,
crew, and passengers were all engaged in vociferous debate
over some fantastic riddle of speculation which lacked all
relevance to either seamanship or the weather. Of course
no one could have foreseen the future, the terrible hurricane already building up in Arabia and destined to break
forth in violence and destruction and to sweep the whole
North, West, and East, as far as the Ebro, the Danube, the
Oxus and the Indus. By contrast, the Western church was
spared the fury of the Muslim conquest, though it ravaged
Sicily and southern Italy, North Africa, and the Iberian
peninsula, and even advanced as far into Gaul as Tours
(in 732) and later swept across Hungary and Austria as
far as the environs of Vienna. The full fury of the conquest
fell upon the Byzantine church and empire. Egypt and
Syria were lost at once, the Patriarchate of Alexandria en-

gulfed and silenced. Hemmed in between the Muslim South
and East and the Gothic North, the Byzantine church was
compelled to content itself with its own internal affairs, as
with a round of "indoor activities"; and so in the East the
vision of a universal empire and a universal church van-
ished, and the church's message became only the words of a
strange, mysterious charm repeated from the past.

Meanwhile, the church in the West moved forward. The
great age of missions had dawned, as Rome undertook to
meet and win over the new northern peoples. The pace was
set by St. Patrick in Ireland and by St. Columba the founder
of Iona, by St. Augustine of Canterbury and St. Wilfred,
Archbishop Theodore of Canterbury, Abbot Aldhelm of
Malmesbury, the Venerable Bede, St. Boniface, the poet
Caedmon—these were among the great figures in the history
of "Northern Catholicism," the memory of whom is still
honored, "for their works do follow them." The result
was the steady growth of territorial or regional churches
(*Landeskirchen*), destined in time to produce distinctive
qualities and characteristics, some of them outstanding and
historically significant. Gallicanism, Anglicanism, Scotch
and Irish Catholicism, even the German and Swiss Reformation were all involved in the future *dénouement* of these
quasi-independent churches. But, in the period we are considering, this very quasi-independence was an asset to the
papacy and strengthened its hand in dealing with the East,
which by now was involved in the Iconoclastic controversy
(Pope Gregory II, 715-31, favored the use of images); and
the final solution, at the Seventh Ecumenical Council, held
at Nicaea in 787, came too late to heal the growing breach
between East and West. For in Rome, Ravenna, and elsewhere the people had revolted against the rule of the Eastern emperor. Gregory III (731-41) had done his best to

repair the breach, but the emperor had replied by severing Thessalonike, Sicily, and all of Byzantine Italy from Rome, making them a part of the Patriarchate of Constantinople, and confiscating the papal lands in these areas.

Yet this very situation was used to advantage by the papacy, astute and resilient as ever. Its hands were now free to deal directly with the greedy Lombards who threatened Rome and the rest of the papal possessions. Gregory III turned to Charles Martel (714-41), who had defeated the Arabs at Tours in 732, and invited him to assume the role of protector of the Tomb of St. Peter, but with no success. In his place, his son Pépin le Bref, "the Short" (741-68), mayor of the palace and king of the Franks and the Germans and founder of the Carolingian dynasty, accepted the invitation of Pope Stephen II (752-7) to intervene and resist the invaders. This was a further stage in the growth of the "papal states," the secular kingdom ruled by the popes in the middle of Italy. It now owed its existence to the king of the Franks. It represented a stage in the history of the papacy, with both positive and negative consequences which endured for more than eleven centuries. It was Pépin's duty to compel the Lombards to yield up the territories they had seized, and to put the exarch of Ravenna in his proper place. The motives of Pépin were unquestionable; but the forces now released, the precedent set for future generations, the worldly status thus conferred upon the papacy, its enduring and inescapable obligations to the Frankish and eventually the French monarchy, the flimsy forgeries that were devised in support of the *fait accompli*, such as the legend of St. Sylvester and the Donation of Constantine—all this was a heritage that lay like Pilgrim's burden on the back of the church for over thirty generations! Even though it led on directly to the brilliant

era of Charlemagne (Charles the Great, 768-814) and the
establishment of the Holy Roman Empire, it was fatal. By
the time of Pope Adrian (772-95) the Franks were the real
rulers of Rome and the popes their underlings. True, Charles
finally subdued the Lombards, but this was incidental to a
wider project: Charlemagne viewed himself as not only
Defensor pacis and *Defensor fidei* ("Defender of the Peace"
and "Defender of the Faith"—many a king has claimed these
titles!), but as the champion of right versus wrong within
the church itself. He was in the direct line of such pious
reformers of the church as Boniface and Pépin. His *Capi-
tularies* set new standards of legislation; his emissaries (*missi
dominici*) attended all church synods. As on a column near
the Spanish Steps in Rome there are two figures, David and
Moses, so Charlemagne viewed himself and the pope as the
two heads of the church-state, one the theocratic ruler, the
other the priestly, whose hands must be upheld in prayer
during the battle (Exodus 17.12). His reforms were significant and far-reaching. The renaissance of learning led by
Alcuin (730-804) was historically important. Finally, his
coronation in Rome by Pope Leo III in the year 800 marked
the final security of the papacy vis-à-vis both the East and
the Romans themselves, and its final release from all obligation to the Eastern court and empire.

But the glory soon departed. The death of Charlemagne
in 814 was followed by the rapid decline of the Frankish
kingdom. Louis the Pious (814-40) and his sons were no
match for either Charles the Great or the enemies that
presently assailed the three kingdoms that now formed the
Holy Roman Empire—roughly France, Italy, and Germany.
The invasions of the Northmen (Normans), the Saracens,
and the Huns were formidable threats. In 846 the Saracens
reached Rome and plundered both St. Peter's and St. Paul's

Outside the Walls. The Huns invaded again and again, pillaging and burning as they went. The Normans attacked the coast of France every year, and finally in 841 made a full-scale invasion. Paris was repeatedly burned.

In these circumstances, the only refuge was, for many, a retreat into fancy. It was during these dark years, in the middle of the ninth century, that the Pseudo-Isidorian Decretals were finally compiled, a conglomeration of false and true decrees, decisions of synods and councils, the Frankish public law, and the Donation of Constantine. The place of the completion of this strange and fantastic compilation was probably Rheims, and the main purpose of the collection was to strengthen the authority of bishops versus councils and metropolitans, and especially to support the authority of the pope, the chief bishop in the West, as a guarantee of the freedom of *all* bishops in the church and of the church itself. This was both Gallicanism and Ultramontanism in one, centuries ahead of time! It was also a distant echo of the episcopalism of St. Cyprian of Carthage (210-58). The authority of synods depended upon papal approval, and all major cases, *causae maiores*, were to be taken to Rome. So even this forgery was useful in its time, and especially two centuries later. A legal fiction if ever there was one, it set forth a principal that was later incorporated in the papal claim to approve or disapprove the acts of all councils, including ecumenical, thus determining or destroying their authority and universality. This principle obviously ruled out the right of the emperor to convene and preside over councils—though the old murals in the Vatican Library still show the Eastern emperor presiding at Nicaea and Constantinople!

As the Carolingian dynasty declined, the papacy rose to meet the situation. Armed with the Pseudo-Isidorian Decre-

tals, and favored by the circumstances of the time, Pope
Nicholas I (858-67) undertook to concentrate the authority
of the church in the papacy, at the expense of the "national"
or "territorial" churches—an idea too early for complete
realization, but destined to fulfilment in the reforms of
the eleventh century. It is denied that the pope himself
engineered the project, and especially the forgery of the
decretals, or their use. Whoever the author, the result was
the same. The forgeries were not detected—at least not
unmasked—until the seventeenth century, when the reformer David Blondel (d. 1655) proved them false. But
alas, the destiny that overtook the monarchy also overtook
the papacy. One result of the following weak succession
of popes was the renewed rift between East and West
(in 867), a schism that certainly rested upon trivial grounds
—almost as trivial as those in the time of Acacius and Zeno
the Isaurian (484-519) and the so-called *Henotikon* (482).[5]
Some of the friction of the earlier schism still survived,
and more was added. Of course the basic cause was the
total shift in orientation of the West, from Byzantium and
the Eastern empire to the Franks and the North, and the
new "Holy" Roman Empire. But for the ninth century the
major issues were theological. The Eastern church still
rejected the sabbath fast, the use of milk, butter, cheese
during the first week of Lent, the obligation of priestly
celibacy—these were old issues; it also rejected the separation of confirmation from baptism, and the use of the term
filioque in the creed. At the Third Council of Constantinople (869), the controversy was presumably settled.
Photius of Constantinople (already pronounced deposed
by a Roman synod in 863) was now officially declared
deposed and excommunicated by an ecumenical council—

5. Bettenson, pp. 123-6. Cross, p. 621 ("Henoticon").

though the East has never recognized it as ecumenical. But he rallied his forces, claimed restoration, and was not finally put out until 886. Thus the deep alienation of East and West settled down for good or for ill and reached its final conclusion in the Great Schism of 1054.

By the year 900, the whole West was in full decline. Worst of all was the condition of the West Frankish Kingdom, where the nobility now began to seize cloisters and churches and their lands, and where monastic discipline all but disappeared. Lay abbots with wives, children, and armed retainers took over the monasteries. Almost as bad were the conditions in the East Frankish Kingdom, though here the bishops and the monarch took a stand against the plundering nobility. And in Italy, one of the darkest periods in papal history began: the popes were dependent upon the noble families and freely engaged in their internecine conflicts. Certain powerful women ruled Rome: e.g. Theodora, wife of the "senator" Theophylact. She was thought to be the mistress of Pope John X (914-28), whose election she had engineered. Her daughter Marozia married a foreign mercenary, Alberic, who supported Theophylact and also the pope. In the war with the Saracens in Sicily—they had captured Taormina in 902 and put to death every resident, but were defeated on the Garigliano in 916—Theophylact and Alberic led the Roman forces. Thereupon both men disappeared. But Marozia was soon remarried, this time to Hugo, Margrave of Tuscany. The pope she imprisoned in Castel Sant' Angelo (in 928) where he was murdered—by order of the daughter of the woman who had raised him to the papal throne! In 931 she made her son Alberic the new pope, John XI. The story continues, long and entangled; but enough has been related to indicate the depth to which the papacy, the whole country, Western Christendom and Western civilization had descended early in the tenth century. The ancient titles survived, but the government of Italy was only an empty shadow of its classical achievement.

In the North, the Danes were sweeping the coasts of England; but a heroic king, Alfred the Great, stood firm, resisted, and succeeded in restoring Christianity and Anglo-Saxon culture. In the lowering darkness that now gathered over all of Europe, England alone possessed a church which had escaped the decline into barbarism. It was the darkest hour; all the earth was "full of darkness and cruel habitations"; but this darkest hour came, as often, just before the dawn.

IV

The Papacy at the Height
of Its Power: 900-1300

The popular conception of church history as the steady, effortless unrolling of a long series of events, smooth as the ripples on a widening stream, each age an advance beyond its predecessor, each council a further unfolding of divine truth as contemporary need, inquiry, or error demanded, slow and steady as the rolling down of some magic curtain covered with picturesque scenes from the past— this common conception is almost nauseating to a student trained in historical research and familiar with the sources. It presupposes the stupid, misleading "triumphalism" frequently deplored by the Council Fathers at Vatican II. Instead, church history was just as dramatic as secular history—in fact, much of it *was* secular, and the church occupied an enormous sector within the secular process. It would really be better to begin the study of church history by assuming that it was all secular: any other conclusion can be based on the evidence, when the time comes. There were situations when the whole outlook appeared hopeless, when the battle was all but lost; suddenly from somewhere came unanticipated succor, a *volte face*, a flank

movement, a new resource, a leader matched to the crisis
of the time. If Protestants have looked for God's "judg-
ments" in history, and have found them in the reverses
suffered by the papacy and the papal church, it is also possible to look deeper and discover divine rescues, saving acts,
interpositions, so that God's "salvation" also belongs to the
story. It is really a bright *Heilsgeschichte*, a "Story of
Salvation," and not merely a long tale of doom. Just in the
nick of time, the papacy freed itself from the slackening
hand of Byzantine dominion; just in the nick of time,
Clovis was converted, and the papal alliance was formed
with the Franks, thus guaranteeing the freedom and security of the church in Rome and Italy; just in the nick of
time, Charles the Great became emperor—a huge achievement, a turning point in history, weak as were his successors, and purely theoretical as the church-state alliance was
destined to be during most of the early decades of the Holy
Roman Empire.

It is this modern, human, basically secular view of the
papacy that makes the story far more interesting—and
true. It also yields the institution a much higher spiritual,
moral, and intellectual rating than the old-fashioned juve-
nile, apologetic, story-book tale ever did. Instead of a slow,
dull, plodding effort, pope after pope, to achieve the golden
dream of St. Peter and all his successors, viz. a world dominion for the Vicar of Christ in the best interest of all
nations, we now see the human factors involved, and the
human weakness displayed, and the swift, brilliant strokes
of genius, of born administrators and tacticians, following
a common strategy but adapting the stroke, the deed, the
decision to suit the event. It has been said that the papacy,
like elephants and women, "never learns anything, never
forgets anything," and the saying is partly true. Certainly

the papacy never forgot its main, over-arching, strategic aim—except during certain dismal, degenerate days in the fifteenth and sixteenth centuries. Certainly it never learned timidity, or a paralyzing caution, as when "the burnt child avoids the fire." "Through good report and ill report," in weakness and in strength, in days of prosperity and also of adversity, these very Christian leaders plodded on, valiant to the end, and loyal to an idea, which, misconceived as it was in some respects, nevertheless enshrined one of the noblest ideals ever imagined, that is, the unity, peace, and welfare of mankind, both its spiritual and its material welfare, under the banner of Christ and his one true church. All the Christian churches have benefited by this dream, and by its partial fulfilment hitherto; so have the nations, whatever their religion. Its full and final achievement still lies in the future, a realization which will doubtless modify the terms in which hitherto it has been envisioned and described (this is true of all fulfilments of prophecy!), but it will really transcend rather than fall short of the too-human patterns heretofore anticipated or devised.

The eight centuries from the fifth to the thirteenth were the most crucial in the whole history of the papacy. What followed, from the thirteenth to the twentieth, was fully conditioned by what went before. The popular idea that the modern papacy is the result of various movements and events such as the Renaissance, the Reformation, the Counter Reformation, the *Aufklärung* or Enlightenment, and the European Revolutions, is only partially true. The movements and events of the past four hundred years have affected, but only slightly, an institution already formed and mature by 1300. The *making* of the Roman papacy belongs to the period from 500 to 1300. Itself emerging out of the ruins of Hellenistic Roman civilization in the West, and

sharing in the rise of a new and revived society, aided by
the resurgence of letters, law, and learning, and at the same
time contributing greatly to the resurgence, the papacy did
more than any other monarchy in Europe, more than any
other organization or society on earth, to foster the new
civilization that emerged in the fifteenth to eighteenth
centuries, and still survives, though now threatened with
decline, or indeed with eclipse, by completely amoral and
purely "scientific" materialism.

The four centuries from 900 to 1300 saw the transition
from the old Carolingian theory of church and state, with
the king or emperor acting as guardian of Peter's tomb and
ally of the pope, to the completely new idea of the independent church, with the pope at its head, superior to the
state and assigning duties to the royal heads or conceding
whatever rights they were allowed. It was the age that
began with the total collapse of the Carolingian tradition
and culture, and with gross corruption of the church in
Rome, followed almost at once by the Cluniac reform,
Hildebrand's (Gregory VII's) application of its principles
on every level, the Investiture Controversy and its conclusion, the crusades, the intellectual achievements of Scholasticism, and the establishment of the Holy Inquisition.
But the unceasing cycle continued: success bred decline,
and the fourteenth century marked a decided lowering of
church life and thought, practice and theory, in almost
every direction. And that in turn led to further developments, including efforts at reform, as we shall see.

The emperor Otto the Great (936-73), son of the German King Henry the Fowler, saw clearly the impossibility
of resting his throne upon the nobility; he turned to the
church, i.e. to the bishops and abbots. Exercising his ancient
royal right as king of Germany, he made the heads of the

church into a spiritual nobility, and loaded them with land and wealth, to such a degree that they could look down on the hereditary nobles. No longer was the church in danger of the seizure of its property by land-hungry or rapacious nobles; this arrangement also guaranteed the security of the throne for a century and more, until the reign of Henry IV (1056-1106). The political device was simple—and old. Martin Nilsson's caption for the control of religion by the successors of Alexander the Great could be used here: "Religion in the service of the kings." It proved fatal, in time, when the pope placed a ban upon the king, and the bishops deserted him and flocked to support the pope. But while it worked the theory was a great success. Similar conditions were found elsewhere, as in England later on when the ecclesiastical nobility brought into the royal service the best brains, and the best educated, leaving the parishes and dioceses and monasteries to get on as best they could. For a time it looked as if the Ottonian device would even revive the papal prestige. The tenth century was a very dark period in Rome, and Otto did all an emperor could do to reform the papacy, and also to secure his own coronation as Holy Roman emperor (in 962) by a worthy pope. He clearly looked back to the great days of Charlemagne, and undertook to carry on his principles of administration and of relations with the church. So did his successors, Otto II and Otto III, the latter in full earnest: as a symbol, he translated the bones of Charlemagne to Aachen in the year 1000. Incidentally, he held the Donation of Constantine to be a forgery—evidence that not everyone accepted that fiction, though its popularity is evident enough. The famous series of paintings in the old mediaeval church of Santi Quattro Coronati on the Coelian Hill in Rome illustrates the whole fiction of Pope Sylvester and Constantine. What Dante thought of it is clear from *Inferno* 19.115ff.

> *Ahi, Constantin, di quanto mal fu matre,*
> *non la tua conversion, ma quella dote*
> *che da te prese il primo ricco patre!*

(Alas, O Constantine, how much evil was born, not from your conversion but from that fatal gift the first rich Father received from you!)

But the tenth century also introduced the beginning of one of the most vigorous efforts at reform in all church history. The monastery of Cluny in Burgundy was headed for two centuries by a series of abbots who were pledged to reform their own order and also monastic life generally throughout the empire. Their policy, originating with Odo (927-42) and formulated by Odilo, who was abbot for fifty-five years (994-1049), was to increase the wealth and security of the cloister, free it from the oppressive control of the bishop and place it directly under the pope, strengthen its discipline, which was based on the Benedictine Rule, and lay more emphasis on the religious life—devotion, piety, and self-denial. Cluny became the headquarters of the first truly centralized monastic order. The reform spread in all directions. In Italy it resulted in an enormous wave of asceticism, led by such a zealous reformer as Peter Damiani (1007-72). At the same time the movement shifted its objective from personal religion and monastic discipline to the reform of the church as a whole, aimed especially at the two evils of simony (the purchase of "preferment" or advancement in ecclesiastical status) and concubinage. Obviously the movement was headed in a direction that would lead eventually to collision with the emperor.

Meanwhile, a noble pope, Leo IX (1049-54) espoused the cause of reform and applied it directly to the papacy. Canonical requirements were established and observed. Regular synods were held. The pope visited various parts of the church outside Rome. The College of Cardinals was made into a papal court or Curia. But the pope overstepped the limits, and engaged in a struggle with the Normans in southern Italy. He was captured by them in 1053 and was released only upon cancellation of the ban he had imposed upon them. Seizing the opportunity, and seeking to recover lost ground and gain favor for the Greeks in southern Italy, the patriarch of Constantinople, Michael Caerularius (1043-59), now revived the ancient dispute with Rome. Leo at once sent his messengers to Constantinople with a ban, which they laid on the high altar of Hagia Sophia on July 16, 1054. The Byzantine authorities immediately replied to this contemptuous—and contemptible—act, and the Great Schism between East and West began, a schism not healed to this day. Thus the rashness even of good men can produce great evil.

The emperor Henry III (1039-56) also favored reform and, paradoxically, thus did more to encourage a desire for the true freedom of the church than any fanatical ecclesiastic could possibly have succeeded in doing. Alas, he died at thirty-nine, when his son, Henry IV, was only six. Nothing much happened for almost twenty years, though the papal power, now enlisted in reform, was quietly building up its strength and preparing to free itself, when the time came, from imperial control. By this time another heroic figure had emerged upon the scene, the Tuscan monk Hildebrand, later to become Pope Gregory VII, already deeply committed to the ideals of Cluniac reform. And a pope had arisen, Nicholas II (1059-61), who in his first year, at Easter 1059, issued a decree that the choice of a pope should rest henceforth, not with the Roman nobility, nor with the emperor, but with the cardinal bishops. The other clergy and the laity could either confirm or reject the choice—or merely protest. Something had to be added to "save the honor" of the emperor, and so the words were subjoined: *salvo debito honore et reverentia dilecti filii nostri Henrici regis.*[1] But no one knew quite what this reservation of royal privilege or honor amounted to. The forces of reform were closing in.

Meanwhile, also, various political alliances were effected, e.g. in southern Italy, where the papacy now reconciled itself with the Normans and handed over to them most of Apulia, Calabria, and Capua—at the expense of the emperor. (The Normans were of course subject as vassels to the pope.) The old gateway to the South, on the shore road a few miles north of Naples, is still there: it was the entrance to these new estates of the church. In turn the Normans were given a free hand to conquer Sicily, retaking it from the Saracens, and also to seize England (in 1066). Conceivably, the latter invasion was designed to keep England and Scotland from falling into the hands of the Vikings. But King Harold was fully prepared to do this; he successfully resisted them before turning south to face the Normans under William the Conqueror, at Hastings. This time Harold was defeated. The ravaging and destruction of old Saxon churches and monasteries, the "harrowing of the North" (not a man, woman, child, or beast was left alive in Yorkshire), and the burning of Alcuin's library at York (the best library in northern Europe), were inexplicable and

1. Mirbt, § 270.

unforgivable. The Normans were still barbarians, only one step above the savage Vikings. Their architecture, destined to be influential, was as much military as ecclesiastical: witness Durham Cathedral, offset by Kelso Abbey farther north.

Hildebrand became pope in 1073, and in twelve years he placed a stamp on the Christian church in the West, on the papacy, and on the political institutions of Europe, one that is still visible after almost nine centuries. He was the avowed champion of the Cluniac reform. He enforced clerical celibacy and put down simony. He wholly identified the interests of the papacy with those of the Catholic church. He furthered the unification and Romanizing of the church throughout western Europe. Above all, he took away the rights of kings and emperors to "invest" bishops and archbishops with either their spiritual or their temporal responsibilities. This last was a frontal attack on the prerogatives enjoyed by the Frankish and German kings since the days of Charlemagne, and long before. Indeed, it was a sacred prerogative of the old Saxon kings, widely spread throughout Europe, and was supposed to be in accordance with the law of Christ and the custom of the Romans, as seen for a long time past in the usage of Byzantium.

The best statement of his principles is the *Dictatus Gregorii Papae*,[2] twenty-seven brief theses on the Rights of the Pope which he wrote (or dictated) in 1075, the second year of his reign. Its main points were these: (1) The pope is the sole ruler of the universal church; he alone can depose or transfer metropolitans and bishops; he alone (not the emperor) can call a general council; his legates are superior in rank to bishops—these last two points are

2. Mirbt, § 278; Denzinger omits.

still to be made out relatively to the early Greek councils, especially Nicaea, and even Chalcedon.

(2) He bears the imperial insignia (the crown, not yet the triple tiara); his feet, not the bishops', must be kissed by princes in token of their submission; he can even depose the emperor and release his subjects from their oath of allegiance—a device that was still attempted in the days of Queen Elizabeth I.[3]

(3) He stands under the special protection of St. Peter; thanks to the merits of that Apostle, the canonically chosen pope is undoubtedly "holy," i.e. a sacred person. Accordingly, the *Roman* church has been preserved from all error, and will continue to be so preserved.

The authenticity of the *Dictatus* has been questioned, and it has been thought to be a clerk's later summary of Gregory's views. But the twenty-seven articles all refer to conditions which were to be found in the troubled opening years of his pontificate, especially the involved and most difficult international situation, chiefly vis-à-vis the German emperor Henry IV, and Gregory may well have outlined and defined the principles upon which he intended to stand. Gregory had enemies even within the Curia (Hugo Candidus), and the higher ranks of the German clergy were opposed; some renounced their allegiance. Young Henry even pronounced the pope's deposition and ordered the Romans to elect a new pontiff. This is a part of the background of Canossa not often stressed in popular accounts of the pope's triumph. The later principles and policies of Pope Gregory well illustrate the brief formulations of the *Dictatus*.

Relying on an Old Testament text (Jer. 48.10, "Cursed is he who keeps back his sword from bloodshed"), Gregory

3. See Bettenson, pp. 338f.

concluded that a merciless war of extinction should be launched against the enemies of St. Peter and for the rights and liberty of holy church. He believed himself to be fighting for pure *justitia*, and his fanaticism knew no bounds; any weapon would serve: ban, interdict, excommunication, or appeal to the masses to revolt. Even some of the reformers boggled at this.

His great struggle was with Henry IV (1050-1106) on the question of Lay Investiture, but the real end in sight was the complete domination of the whole world-church. The popular religion of the time was on his side, and in every country he found supporters. In 1074 he laid down the new requirements for celibacy, deposing those of the clergy who failed to obey—to the great consternation of the laity, whose sacraments were now to be administered by invalid hands. A year later he advanced the next step, and forbade lay investiture. The result of this was the removal of all imperial control over the bishops; from being princes and potentates in the empire, an ecclesiastical nobility surrounding the king, they were at once set free (and their estates with them) to become "princes of the church." One more year (1076) and he released the emperor's subjects from their oaths of allegiance to the now excommunicate King Henry. The result was social and political chaos, and it brought Henry to his knees—in the snow at Canossa, January 25-28, 1077.[4] Another view is that Canossa was a clever device by which Henry forced the pope to show his hand, and grant absolution, thereby preventing encirclement on his own ground—in the Diet of the princes at Augsburg. But this is a highly speculative interpretation. The pope lifted the ban, but the question

4. Mirbt, § 280.

remained whether or not and to what extent Henry was
still emperor.

Here was one more turning point in European history.
Though the pope apparently won, the reaction and the
resentment his victory aroused were far-reaching. The
northern nations never forgot the scene, the barefoot king
kneeling in the snow, begging to be reinstated for the sake
of the peace and well-being of his people—and his own.
The picture may not be accurate in detail—the bared feet
and the snow—but it was essentially and in principle correct,
and this is what men remembered. The drift toward independent national churches was destined to grow stronger
with every century from now on. The pope had over-
played his hand, and there was no possibility of retrieving
the terrible blunder of Canossa. In fact, to this very day
this image reappears in every discussion of Roman Catholic
relations to politics, national governments, and even city
elections. The POAU (Protestants and Other Americans
United for the Separation of Church and State) are easily
able to raise this ghost on any appropriate occasion.

Henry died in 1106, twenty-one years after Gregory
VII (d. 1085). Their battle continued throughout that
generation, and even longer. The papal claim to world-
dominion was tacitly dropped, and the popes contented
themselves with denouncing lay investiture. Under Urban
II (1088-99), Henry undertook to enthrone an antipope,
Clement III, and to win for him recognition in Germany;
but the plan fell through. The crowning achievement of
the period was Urban's proclamation of the first crusade at
the Council of Clermont in 1095. This herring, skillfully
drawn across the trail, altered the situation completely.
The people responded "as one man," and from now on the

pope was head of western Christendom, leading its hosts against the common enemy in the Holy Land. The many political leaders and demagogues who have resorted to some such device clutter the byways of history.

The climax and seal of the victory came at the First Lateran Council, in 1123, when the German emperor lost every right to invest, either with episcopal ring or pastoral staff, the bishops in his realm, though he still claimed homage for their feudal estates. The victory came earlier in England (1106), when Anselm of Canterbury compelled the Norman king, William Rufus, to renounce all rights to investiture. And victory it certainly was. Henceforth all royal claims to rights over the church, though often made, were rejected in advance. From now on, the popes had canon law, precedent, and newly established custom on their side, as against all ancient rules among the Franks, the Carolingians, the Saxons, and the Salian kings, or, farther afield, the Eastern Roman emperors. The victory was more than a personal one for the papacy; it meant the spiritual freedom of the church from control by earthly monarchs, from purchase and sale or barter, from the promotion of favorite sons and political aspirants or supporters—at least in theory. But this freedom could also be abused, even in papal hands. *Corruptio optimi pessima*—"the corruption of the best often results in the worst."

There were seven crusades during the two centuries from 1096 to 1291, each one—after the third—more futile, cruel, and inexcusable than the last. The ostensible purpose was the recovery of the "holy places" in Palestine from the "infidel," i.e. the Muslims. The occupation of these sites by the Arabs from 636 onward was scandal enough, and the fees they charged pilgrims who came to visit the sacred

sites were outrageous; but the seizure of Palestine in 1072
by the Seljuk Turks, wild nomads from central Asia, was
insupportable, especially when they refused admission to
pilgrims on any terms. The Eastern emperor Alexius I
Comnenus (1081-1118) appealed to the pope for help in
facing the new foe. Tales of returning pilgrims fanned the
flame, and all western Europe was eager to drive out the
Turk. A strong appeal was made by Urban II at the Council of Clermont, where he addressed a vast open-air meet-
ing. "It is the will of God," the multitude shouted back:
Deus lo vult!—and thousands of Frenchmen enlisted for the
holy war. By New Year 1096 a motley multitude of hood-
lums and adventurers got under way, several months before
the organized expedition of knights was ready to depart.
These wild freebooters, lured by the prospect of loot and
adventure in the fabulous East and urged on by the economic pressure at home, made their undisciplined scramble
up the Rhineland, across Switzerland, and on toward the
East. Their record was infamous. Every Jewish house they
came upon was looted and burned; every Jewish woman
was raped and murdered; every Jewish child and man was
tortured and put to death. All this in the name of religion
and with the blessing of the church! It is the darkest chapter
in all church history, and it refutes the theory that a "little"
war can be a good thing and that bloodshed is normal in
human behavior. The final result, three years later, when
first Antioch and then Jerusalem fell before the armed
crusaders, was only a hollow victory—at best only a part
of western Asia Minor and the seacoast of Syria were freed
from "the infidel"; the rest of the East remained Muslim
and Turkish, as before. The mixed multitude of thieves,
bandits, and murderers who preceded the army had been

wiped out in Bulgaria and on the plain of Nicaea. The friction with the Byzantines, especially on the part of the
Norman knights, was a sad commentary on the promised
aid to the Eastern church, and all too patently, already in
the First Crusade as in those that followed, the secret aim
of the papacy, viz. to conquer the East and bring the Eastern church into subjection to Rome, had simply miscarried.
The Greeks wanted help, and needed it desperately; but
there was one price too high to pay, submission to the
West.

For two centuries now, romantic historians and novelists
have described the crusades in glamorous terms. Modern
historians see the sordid side, the futility and shame of the
whole performance. Nevertheless, some of the results were
positive; the economic and social consequences of this close
contact with the East were noteworthy. New demands for
commodities obtainable only in the East, and unknown
since Roman days (for example, pepper), now stimulated
trade and advanced the interests of the middle class. And
the very churches, with their colored murals and windows,
henceforth reflected the world of bright color the crusaders
had seen in Syria and Palestine. Moreover, the papacy, having sponsored the movement, likewise profited by it. The
trade in relics and the sale of indulgences expanded—to die
for the faith, on a crusade, guaranteed full remission of
penance; the failure of the crusades was not apparent until
long after. In the meantime, the popes, as leaders of the
whole West, prospered, just as the ruling class often does
during a war, however disastrous its consequences for the
people. But the fatal aftermath, the historical nemesis, eventually caught up with them. It is not the business of spiritual leaders to start wars and to rally, recruit, and launch
armies.

The powerful movement for monastic and clerical reform that began at Cluny in 910 had results that continued
for centuries. Other orders were founded, some even more
rigid in their observance of the monastic rule of life: for
example, the Augustinians (1059), the Cistercians (1098),
and the Praemonstratensians (1120). The military orders
of St. John and the Templars (both in 1120) were designed
to protect and care for pilgrims to the Holy Land. There
was even an order of unarmed "Hospitalers," the Order of
St. Anthony (from about 1095). Monastic piety was reflected at its noblest in such a figure as Bernard of Clairvaux
(1091-1153), who has been described by Karl Heussi with
epitaphic brevity: "The religious genius of the twelfth century, counsellor of popes, prince of the uncrowned rulers
of Europe." He even rebuked the worldliness and the
worldly aims and claims of the papacy in his book *On
Consideration*, dedicated to Pope Eugenius III who had
been his pupil. One must also mention the Victorines,
monks of the famous Abbey of St. Victor at Paris, whose
views resembled Bernard's, and who combined ardent piety
and personal devotion to Christ (like that of Bernard) with
a metaphysical mysticism based on the writings of the fifth-
century author wrongly identified with Dionysius the
Areopagite (Acts 17.34). In fact, the influence perhaps
worked the other way around: Bernard was greatly influenced by Hugh of St. Victor. This type of theology was
new; instead of being based upon tradition and syllogism,
it rested upon the analysis of direct religious experience of
a mystical type, something it owed directly to Abelard
(1079-1142), even though Bernard rejected Abelard's dia-
lectic, his too rigidly logical type of reasoning.

At the same time, the revival of the church's spiritual life

resulted in an enormous missionary movement, in Poland,
Germany, Scandinavia, Hungary, and Russia. The revival
was also reflected in the beginnings of Scholasticism, e.g.
in the work of Anselm of Canterbury (1033-1109). His
rigorous "ontological argument" for the existence of God
(*quo maius cogitari non potest*: "than Whom no greater
can be conceived") survived for seven centuries, until the
publication of Immanuel Kant's *Critique of Pure Reason*
in 1781 (Kant may have missed the point, that the ground
of being cannot be conceived as non-existent); and his
theory of the Atonement, as an act of restitution or satisfaction (*satisfactio*) made to the affronted honor of God, has
survived for longer still. The philosophical foundation of
this earlier Scholasticism of the eleventh and twelfth centuries was basically classical: the Realists, who believed that
"universals" exist apart from their manifestation in con-
crete things, followed Plato, as he was understood and
interpreted by Neoplatonists and others; the Nominalists,
who insisted that "universals" exist only in the mind, which
uses them in classifying its own experience of external
things, followed Aristotle, as understood at the time. This
knowledge of Aristotle was mediated by a long, circuitous
route: Syriac translations of the Greek works of Aristotle
were translated into Arabic by Muslim scholars, and the
Arabic was in turn translated into Latin in Spain and elsewhere, as Arabic learning and philosophy came to be
known through the Moors. But by 1215 fresh manuscripts
of the Greek originals of Aristotle's writings were brought
to the West, including his larger works on Logic and
Ethics; these were promptly translated into Latin. Nevertheless, the foundations of mediaeval philosophy had been
well and truly laid by the scholars of the eleventh and

twelfth centuries, during the so-called "Twelfth-Century Renaissance," and so the work of the great leaders of the thirteenth-century High Scholasticism was made possible. Realism prevailed. Nominalism was condemned at the Council of Soissons in 1092, but survived *sub rosa*, and was revived by William of Ockham in the fourteenth century.

This was the world at the beginning of the high Middle Ages, a world teeming with energy, full of conflict, determination, vitality. Bernard's preaching had led to a second crusade (1147-9), which ended in total failure before the walls of Damascus, but not before damaging still more the broken relations with the Eastern church. Bernard was now viewed as a false prophet. This tragedy was scarcely ended before the second act in the long drama of conflict between the empire and the papacy began. Frederick I, "Barbarossa" ("Red Beard," 1152-90), undertook to recover the ancient rights of the German crown, inspired not by Henry IV's example but by the East Roman concept of empire as set forth in the legislation of Justinian, which was now studied in the Western schools of law. Opposed to him were the Roman Curia, firmly rooted in the conception of church and state that had been expounded and defended by Gregory the Great, and renewed and reinforced by Gregory VII. The new pope, Alexander III (1159-81) led the defense of papal rights against the emperor, and turned the defense into a victory. His chief weapon was the ban and the interdict, by which he released Frederick's subjects from their allegiance. At the peace of Venice (1177) the emperor withdrew his support of the antipope Victor IV and acknowledged Alexander III. Another ruler, Henry II of England and France, was compelled to do penance and receive punishment at the tomb of his enemy, Archbishop Thomas à Becket, whom Henry's Norman knights had murdered in 1170—only then would the papal ban be lifted. Thanks to the intervention of the pope, Henry's attempt to dominate the English church was a total failure. Though Alexander was himself long an exile from Italy, he returned in time to convene the Third Lateran Council in 1179,[5] the council which undertook to end papal schisms by a decree that henceforth papal elections must be decided by a two-thirds majority of all the Roman cardinals, not just the cardinal bishops, as in the bull of Nicholas II in 1059. From now on the appointment of imperial antipopes was— in theory—impossible! But again the Roman opposition to the pope broke forth, and Alexander died in exile at Civita Castellana in 1181.

Thus defeat and victory were mingled in almost equal parts, but, like the British army as described in a famous saying, the papacy seemed to "lose every battle but the last." Frederick Barbarossa set forth on the Third Crusade in 1189, but died in Asia Minor, on his way to the Holy Land. For centuries the legend survived that he, like *Nero redivivus*, was only sleeping in a cave somewhere in the East, and would return at the head of a great army and right all wrongs, at least those suffered by his still credulous supporters. His son, Henry VI (1190-97), undertook to carry forward his father's policies and place all Italy under the emperor's control. This time fate—or the Hand of God —intervened, and Henry died young, at thirty-two, leaving the throne to his three-year-old son Frederick II. The imperial power in Italy shrank, and the two Sicilies were immediately lost by the empire.

5. Mirbt, § 316.

The long struggle between empire and papacy, which was the "modern" history reflected in Dante's writings, was like a game of basketball or hockey between two well-matched teams. The contest surged from goal to goal; one generation seemed to see the end, as the victor stood before the opposing goal. Suddenly the scene changed, and the battle surged in the opposite direction. So now a skillful leader, Pope Innocent III (1198-1216), at once seized the advantage and aroused the slumbering loyalties of the Western nations. Not world rule, indeed, but the central and dominating position in world politics, was the aim and the achievement of this great pope with his genius for leadership. Italy, both central and southern, and Sicily, like Rome itself, were bound more firmly to the papal throne; the imperial authority was made subservient to the ecclesiastical; his external policies, e.g. in England, and even in the East, were crowned with success; and the dangerous heretics in southern France, the Cathari, were put down. True, he opposed the English barons' *magna carta libertatum* in 1215, which they wrung from the reluctant King John;[6] what Innocent wanted was not the principle, *ecclesia anglicana libera sit* ("Let the English church be free"), which might be misinterpreted and carried too far, but a total submission of both church and state to the papal rule—a simple reversal of Henry's attempt to enforce the *Constitutions of Clarendon* (1164).[7] Another defeat was the Fourth Crusade (1202-4), aimed directly at the conquest of the Eastern church. Constantinople was taken and a "Latin Empire" set up in place of the Byzantine monarchy, but it was short-lived (until 1261), and during these

6. Bettenson, pp. 226-32.
7. Bettenson, pp. 220-26.

sixty years the Eastern churches continued in stubborn opposition to the papal rule.

Nevertheless, the reign of Innocent closed in splendor. The Fourth Lateran Council (1215) was attended by over 2000 members, and dealt chiefly with the reform of the church and the liberation of the Holy Land. The decree defining the doctrine of Transubstantiation was far-reaching in its consequences. It was a noble attempt to define the indefinable, and a brilliant solution of a problem in philosophy, granted the new Scholastic-Aristotelian physics and the terms it used (*substantia, materia, forma, accidens*, etc.); but it was no longer adequate, once science had moved on to new conceptions of physical reality—though the basic idea may still be as good as any to *symbolize* and interpret what modern physics has to say about the nature of things. Other decrees defined the rights of episcopal inquisition, dealt with auricular confession, and forbade any further founding of religious orders—a rule that was promptly forgotten! But the magnificence of this council and its display of papal authority and power was only a fleeting demonstration: the financial drain upon the nations, the scandal of nepotism, and the purely political machinations of the papacy aroused widespread and lasting criticism. There were already, two hundred years before Luther, those who did not hesitate to call the pope "Antichrist." Reform, much farther-reaching than that of Cluny, was already in the air. The glories and achievements of the thirteenth century were real enough, in art, architecture, philosophy, poetry, piety, religious missions and propaganda. Even the Inquisition might be included: it was designed to hold all in order! But the increasing entanglement in secular affairs, for example, in the later crusades and even in the two councils of Lyons (1245, 1274),

marked the beginning of a swift decline from the peak
of achievement already won. The struggle between the
popes and the Hohenstaufen was over, and the popes were
victorious, though at some cost in prestige; but before the
thirteenth century was out the fatal dependence of the
papacy upon the support of the French nobility was becoming clearer every day. The poetry of Dante, and his political views, were representative and exemplary: everyone
appreciated the former; the latter steadily won converts.
A worldly papacy was henceforth a contradiction in terms.

The period ended like others, with a vast and growing
menace counterbalancing all past achievements and present
power. The last crusade (1291) was a complete and ghastly
failure. The "Latin Kingdom" in Constantinople had fallen
in 1261. In 1291 the Muslim forces crushed the military
orders in Palestine, which now began their long retreat
homeward to Cyprus, Rhodes, Venice, Malta, and East
Prussia. But in 1261, when Constantinople was regained by
the Eastern emperor Michael VIII Palaeologus, ruler of the
Kingdom of Nicaea, the restored empire possessed only a
shadow of its former power. In 1274 he signed a political
Union with the Roman church, but it was promptly
opposed and repudiated by the Greek people and soon fell
into desuetude. As the curtain began to come down on the
thirteenth century, the Mongol power, Genghis Khan and
his hordes, moved ever closer to the West. Northern Iran
and southern Russia were already in their possession, and
northern Russia was now dependent upon the "Kingdom
of the Golden Horde" (1240-1480). The Nestorians in
Middle Asia were almost exterminated, and so were the
Jacobites and the Armenians. But again, as always, a new
and brighter day was about to dawn.

The view, widespread a generation ago, that Christianity

reached its religious and cultural climax in the thirteenth century, since when it has slowly declined, is surely a view based upon more enthusiasm than knowledge. Nevertheless, the external evidence supporting it is still strong and cannot be disregarded or explained away.

V

The Renaissance: 1300-1500

There are various theories of the course of history, theories derived mainly from mechanical processes, e.g. the swing of a pendulum, a cyclical rotation, a spiral, the ebb and flow of the tide. There are also those who hold that history has no pattern, as H. A. L. Fisher stated in the introduction to his *History of Europe*. Among the oldest theories is the one found in the Book of Judges: "The people of Israel again did what was evil in the sight of the Lord; and the anger of the Lord was kindled against Israel, and he sold them into the hand of the Philistines.... And the Lord delivered them"—when they repented (see Judges 10). One might call this the *wave* theory. The history of the papacy, and of the church in the West, during the long centuries we are considering, was like that; prosperity and reversal alternated in swift sequence. The triumph of the church and its world-wide power under Alexander III and Innocent III gave way to crisis and change, and indeed to the threat of total extinction at the hands of the advancing Mongols. The crisis continued. The later advance of the Turks, to the very "gates of Vienna," like the earlier advance of the Arabs to the Pyrenees and beyond, was another threat to the very existence of Western civilization, the church, and the papacy.

The conditions within the church, especially during the Renaissance, reflected grave internal disunity, weakness, even the symptoms of revolt. The old quarrel between the church and the empire was almost over; the new national groups, nations in the making, took the place of the empire; and the papacy fell into internecine strife, when the "Babylonish Captivity" (1309-77), which lasted for sixty-eight years, was followed by the Great Schism in the West (1378-1415), another thirty-seven years, making a total of one hundred and five years of strife and waste. The various sectarian groups found within the church during the Middle Ages, the Cathari and the Albigensians, the Waldensians, Paulicians, and Bogomils, opened the way for wider defections inaugurated by John Wyclif and led by John Hus. Repeated calls were heard for general councils, and four were actually held: at Vienne in Dauphiné (1311-12), at Constance (1414-18), and at Basel, Ferrara, and Florence (1437-9), followed by the Fifth Lateran Council early in the sixteenth century (1512-17). But as a whole the period was marked by decline from the great days of the twelfth and thirteenth centuries.

The Realist philosophy of the high Middle Ages now gave way to a widespread Nominalism, chiefly as a result of the teaching of William of Ockham (ca. 1300-1349), with its double standard of truth and its doors left wide open to skepticism. Faith and knowledge were set in opposition, providing an apparent escape from unreal dogmatism in theology, but with disastrous consequences that led eventually to a complete and total skepticism. Unfortunately, Ockham's influence survived in Luther, as reflected in his wild and intemperate denunciation of "that devil's whore Reason."[1] A better way of reconciliation was found in mysticism, especially as it was cultivated by the Dominicans in Germany. It marked a pendulum swing away from the acute rationalism of the later Schoolmen, though it swept far to the right in its central emphasis on inner experience, especially of the central dogmas of Christianity. This movement also had a lasting influence, even upon Luther, and survives to this day. The works of Johann Tauler (1300-1361), Heinrich Suso (1295-1366), and Jan van Ruysbroeck (1293-1381) are still read, and also, above all, the beautiful *Theologia Germanica*, written about 1400 by an unknown priest near Frankfort, and edited by Luther in 1516 and 1518. The great mass of the people were not (i.e. not yet) disturbed or roused from their "dogmatic slumbers" or their routine of pious devotion. Pilgrimages, relics, miracles, indulgences, the whole round of secondary devotion continued as before, especially during the terrible three years of the Black Death (1348-51).

As we have seen, the closing years of the thirteenth century found the papacy increasingly subservient to the House of Anjou, now in control of Naples where Boniface VIII (1294-1303) came into conflict with Philip IV of France. Too lightly assuming that his claim to world sovereignty would be effective, the pope suffered a complete reverse; it was obvious that the papal "power" amounted to nothing, politically. As Stalin was to inquire, "How many divisions has the Pope?" It was the French who uncovered both the political and the religious impotence of the papacy. And all this took place at the time of the great Jubilee in Rome (in 1300), which brought countless pilgrims to the Holy City, bearing gifts that immensely

1. Weimar Ausgabe, XVIII, 164, lines 25ff.

enhanced the coffers of the Curia. The totals can only be guessed. Karl Heussi, in his *Kompendium* (§ 65 0), described the sources of the Curia's income, but, like those of the later Rothschilds, the figures were never published, not even a balance sheet; perhaps, again like the Rothschilds, it was unnecessary, as they enjoyed an income too great to count. The revival of trade following the crusades resulted in a wider use of currency; wealth was no longer measured by a few bags of ducats. There was probably more money in circulation now than there had ever been since the third or fourth century.

Philip arrested the papal legate and forced him to face trial when he returned from Italy to his diocese, Pamiers. The pope at once ordered the French hierarchy and scholars to come to Rome for consultation. But the nobility, the clergy, and the people sided with the king. At this the pope issued his famous bull *Unam Sanctam* (1302) [2] which set forth in unmistakable terms the theory of the two swords (Luke 22.38) wielded by the two powers, the spiritual and the secular, and stated that obedience to the Roman pontiff was necessary for salvation: "Henceforth let every human being submit to the Roman pontiff. . . . This is a matter of necessity for salvation" (*porro subesse Romano pontifici omni humanae creaturae . . . omnino esse de necessitate salutis*). Philip appealed to a general council—this was the usual cry of distress in those days—and the pope replied with a ban. But before he could publish it, the king sent a band of armed bravos and shut up the pope in the castle of Anagni (1303). The citizens of Anagni set him free, but he died soon after at Rome. Such was the final collapse of the claim to world-dominion voiced by the

2. Bettenson, pp. 159-61; Denzinger, §§ 870-75; Mirbt, § 372.

papacy at the height of its powers, at the end of the Middle
Ages.

From now on the Curia was chiefly dependent upon the
French throne, and suffered a long political and moral
decline. The first of the Angevin popes was the Gascon
Clement V (1305-14). One of the first acts of his reign
was to charge the dead Boniface VIII with heresy, under
pressure from the French king. Eventually the king was
satisfied with the (presumed) withdrawal of the infamous
bull *Unam Sanctam*. But his action against the Knights
Templar was more serious. The Order had retired to France
after the last crusade, and now held vast estates and other
properties. Its power and influence stood in the way of
royal ambitions, and the king undertook to destroy the
Order, with the aid of the pope. The Grand Master,
Jacques de Molay (1243?-1314), was imprisoned, along
with all Knights Templar living in France, and charged
with heresy and immorality. A papal commission found the
charges false, and so did the Council of Vienne (1311-12).
Nevertheless, their property was seized and, in theory,
turned over to the Knights of St. John; in actuality, it went
to the king and the French nobility. To make the deed
irreversible, de Molay was executed by Philip in 1314.
(Another account states that he was taken before the
French Inquisition and burned at the stake.) To this day,
charges of corruption still hang over the Order of the
Templars: one Roman Catholic scholar has assured me that
they were "rotten." But what can be said of the French
king and the Gascon pope?

Equally unfortunate was the situation in Germany,
where Louis the Bavarian (Louis IV, 1314-47) fought the
last battle between the empire and the papacy. Only the
loyalty of the German nobility saved him from total defeat,

though he died under the papal ban. He likewise appealed to a general council, but in vain. Nevertheless, there were in the German empire by now enough opponents of the popes to support the emperor in his struggle. The new middle class, the city burghers; the Italian Ghibellines; the true Franciscan Minorites, who favored the ancient rule of poverty as against papal luxury; and the authors of a new and revolutionary theory of the kingship, Marsilius of Padua and John of Jandun with their *Defensor Pacis* (1324)—these were arrayed on the king's side. The *Defensor Pacis* [3] based the royal prerogatives explicitly on "the consent of the governed"—it was in reality the ancient German conception of folk sovereignty, with up-to-date anticlerical inferences. The king was not to be subject to the pope, neither were the bishops; nor was the church to be subject to the bishops.

In 1327 Louis went to Rome, had himself crowned by the City Prefect, and at once set up an antipope, Nicholas V (1328-30), who next year took his departure on a fresh crusade. Louis was left trembling for his soul's salvation, considering what he had done. Only in 1338 was the issue cleared, when the German barons (later called electors, *Kurfürsten*) decided that whomever they chose as king should rule, even without papal approval or consent. This decision was promptly sanctioned by the Reichstag at Frankfort, affirming that the one elected to be emperor should be Kaiser *ipso jure*, without any consultation with the pope. The Angevin papacy replied, the year before Louis died, by naming the new king, Charles IV (1346-78); he had purchased the throne by renouncing the rights hitherto claimed by the emperors. His popularity kept him in control for over thirty years. But so great was the ten-

3. Mirbt, § 378.

sion that in 1356 the "Golden Bull" was issued, settling at
last the whole quarrel between the empire and the papacy;
henceforth no papal confirmation or validation of the royal
election was to be required.[4] But even this concession cost
something—other rights had to be ceded to the church. Not
for nothing was Charles IV known as the *Pfaffenkönig*,
the "clerical" king.

The long battle was now over. The new forces in the
field, the power of the laity, the influence of the middle
class, the independence of the landed aristocracy and nobility, the freedom of thought on such subjects as church and
state, led by Marsilius and others—all these new forces were
destined to increase as time went on. The dim "shape of
things to come" was growing clearer every year. The old
world—old as the ancient empire—was breaking up, and
was destined eventually to pass away like the "old cove-
nant" in Hebrews 8.13.

The "Babylonish Captivity" ended in 1377, when Gregory XI re-established the papal residence in Rome. The
sixty-eight year absence of the popes had resulted in chaotic
conditions in Italy. The seven-month reign of Cola di
Rienzi in 1347, first as "Tribune," then as "Augustus,"
with plans for making Rome the center of a revived empire
and a renewed Christianity, came to a swift end under
Clement VI—who, however, bought Avignon from the
Queen of Naples and planned to establish the papacy there
permanently. His successor, Innocent VI (1352-62), undertook to win back the papal states, sending a Spanish cardinal
with an army to recapture them by force. Under these
circumstances it was no wonder that the return of the popes
at once introduced the Great Schism (1378-1415), with

4. On the *Golden Bull,* see James Bryce, *The Holy Roman Empire,*
pp. 234, 243, 471ff.

popes and antipopes at Rome and Avignon dividing the papal authority—and Western Christendom—between them for the next thirty-seven years. It was not so much a conflict between French and Italian interests as between popes and cardinals; but both lines of division were observable. Even the godly were divided! St. Catherine of Siena supported Urban VI; St. Vincent Ferrer supported Clement VII. The consequences of this schism—really a civil war—were disastrous: the bans flung at different rulers by the contending popes left the laity in despair of their personal salvation. If sacraments were invalid, the Christian way of life was impossible. The drain upon the laity by the increasing demands for money—now from two popes and two curias—were colossal. Ever since the "Babylonish Captivity," when the income from the papal states had been interrupted and the popes at Avignon had shifted their demands to a church-wide tax upon the clergy (this had been John XXII's doing, early in the Avignon period), the monetary burden had continued to mount.

Everywhere was heard the cry for reform of the church "in head and members" (Isaiah 1.5-6). The center of the demand was the University of Paris, which was most seriously affected by the international division and rivalry. Here the two professors, Pierre d'Ailly (1350-1420, the "Hammer of Heretics") and Jean de Gerson (1362-?1428), were the leaders in church reform. But much of the force of the demand was channelled off into debate over various possible modes of healing the schism: a general council, or a decision between rival popes, or an appeal to both popes to resign and make way for a new election. More and more strongly, however, rose the demand for a council, not of the emperor and the hierarchy, as in the ancient councils, but of representatives of the whole church, a principle set

forth earlier by Marsilius of Padua. The abortive Council
of Pisa (1409) undertook to set aside both popes (Gregory
XII and Benedict XIII) and elect a third, Alexander V. But
the first two refused to resign, and so now there were
three! Alexander was soon succeeded by the antipope
John XXIII.

A tocsin of revolt was sounded on the distant hills. It
came from John Wyclif (1328-84), an Oxford scholar
whose biblical studies, and especially his translation of the
Bible, made amply clear the wide departure of the papacy
from the "law of God" which he undertook to derive from
Holy Scripture.[5] He went further and denounced later
doctrines (such as transubstantiation) which were not to
be found in scripture, and—worse yet—he sent out his
"poor preachers" to proclaim the pure original gospel.
Wyclif's movement was not the beginning of the Protestant Reformation, but its real harbinger. He has been called
"the morning star of the Reformation." Though strongly
censured, and in constant danger of arrest, he escaped martyrdom. But in 1417 his enemies, acting under the new
Statute *De haeretico comburendo* (1413), burned one of
Wyclif's followers, Sir John Oldcastle, Baron Cobham.

It was in Bohemia that Wyclif's ideas took deepest root.
Here John Hus (1369-1415), a professor at Prague, seized
upon Wyclif's teachings and writings and gave them the
widest possible circulation. Hus's own books were burned,
he was forbidden to preach, a ban was issued against him
and his followers, and in spite of a safe-conduct under
royal guarantee he was seized at the Council of Constance
and burned on July 6, 1415. One might think the degrada-
tion of religious authority had reached its full depth. But

5. Bettenson, pp. 242-51; Denzinger §§ 1151-1230; Mirbt, § 396.

more evils were still in store for the church as its struggled to regain its freedom from ecclesiastical tyranny.

The effort to achieve reform through a general council seemed about to succeed, when first the Council of Constance (1414-18) and later the Council of Basel (1431-49) were convened. But they were manipulated in such a fashion as to neutralize most of the efforts toward reform. The long awaited Council of Constance set itself three tasks: to overcome the scandalous schism of the papacy, to quiet the Wyclifite disturbance, and to reform the church. The first act of manipulation was Pope (i.e. antipope) John XXIII's decision to count votes not by numbers present but by nations, Italian, German, French, and English.[6] The reason—or excuse—was that he lacked a sufficient number of Italians to support him, and that the northern nations were either unfavorable or neutral to his pretensions. In lieu of a fifth "nation" he later added the cardinals, for a fifth vote. Still later the Spanish were added as the fifth. Nevertheless, in spite of such "rigging," the Council achieved its first objective, and John tried to save himself by flight, i.e. in order to avoid having to renounce the papal tiara and thus allow a new election to take place. He assumed that once he had left the scene the Council would dissolve. But the Council continued, thus declaring itself independent of the pope—a clear triumph for "episcopalism" over "curialism." The false pope was seized and dethroned in May 1415. The other two, Gregory XII and Benedict XIII, continued briefly; in 1417 Martin V (John's successor, in the third line of succession) was proclaimed pope and ruled for fourteen years (1417-31). The second important action of the Council was the condemnation of Wyclif's follower, John Hus, who heroically refused to recant on any point

6. Cf. Denzinger, pp. 315f.

and was burned to death the same year (1415). Under the circumstances it is little wonder that the third objective, viz. the reform of the church, got nowhere. It was proposed that regular meetings of the Council should continue to be held (a similar proposal was made in 1962), but the political engagements and entanglements of Martin V blocked all efforts. The political leaders of England, Germany, and France did business with the existing situation, not with some ideal state of affairs only dreamed about by a few theologians or the patient masses of the faithful. In 1418 the Council adjourned, with little to its credit and much to its shame. The dream of conciliar reform was once more postponed. To climax the tragedy, the Hussite wars broke out and central Europe, especially Bohemia, was all aflame.

A second effort was made when the Council of Basel (1431-49) convened. Here the hopes for reform were higher than ever. The scene in the famous painting at Siena of young Enea Sylvio Piccolomini (1405-64) setting forth for the council symbolizes the general expectation: Enea was then an "episcopalist." Like several others, he later turned reactionary, and in 1458 became Pope Pius II. His famous bull, *Execrabilis* (1460),[7] condemned the appeal from a pope to a general council.

The Council of Basel was beset with difficulties from the outset. Almost at once Pope Eugenius IV (1431-47) attempted to dissolve it or transfer it to Italy (Bologna). But the Council refused to dissolve and continued in session in Switzerland; eventually Eugenius had to yield and recognize its continued existence.[8] But the experience strengthened the movement toward democratization. Instead of

7. Denzinger, § 1375; Mirbt, § 406.
8. Cf. Denzinger, p. 330.

four "nations," as at Constance, there were now four "dep-
utations," charged with responsibility for the agenda of the
Council. It was the high-water mark of conciliarism in that
period. One notable action was a reduction in the papal income, which naturally resulted in further tension between
pope and council. The pope now ordered the Council to
adjourn and come to Italy. But again the majority remained
in Basel, and only a minority submitted to the papal order
(1437). In 1438 the rump council convened in Ferrara,
under Eugenius's presidency; the following year it removed
to Florence. By now it included the majority. Meanwhile
the Greeks, who were being hard pressed by the Turks,
sent an urgent appeal for help and offered the West terms
of reunion (1439), which included recognition of the papal
primacy, amelioration of dogmatic differences, mutual recognition of divergent liturgical rites, and the marriage of
the Greek clergy. But the Greek laity would have nothing
to do with this proposed reunion, and promptly rejected
its terms.[9] The compact was only an interesting historical
document (it was recently reprinted by the Mayor of Florence, during the first session of Vatican II); for in 1453
Constantinople fell, and though the pope now tried to rally
a crusade against the Turks, nothing came of it. Thus the
Byzantine Empire and the Byzantine state church both
came to a simultaneous and inglorious end. The church
lived on, but no longer as an organ of the state.

Meanwhile, also, the Council had deposed Pope Eugenius
IV and elected an antipope, Felix V (1439), thereby alien-
ating what remained of any favorable consideration for the
church on the part of the Catholic powers. During the following decade, almost all of the neutrals sided with Pope
Eugenius, and the Council died a slow death. Even so, the

9. Denzinger, §§ 1300-1308.

collapse of the Council was no victory for the Curia. France had formulated the principles of "Gallicanism," and the longing for real reform was still widespread and strong. The true victors in the struggle were the northern nations, which now began to feel their independence.

The last seventy years before the beginning of the Protestant Reformation saw a steady rise in national feeling in the North and West, a deeper entrenchment and resistance on the part of the Roman Curia, and an unprecedented decline in moral and religious power on the part of the papacy. It was the era of the Renaissance popes: Nicholas V, Calixtus III, Pius II, Paul II, Sixtus IV, Innocent VIII, Alexander VI, Pius III, Julius II, Leo X, most of whom were steeped in selfishness and worldliness, and some in lust and vice. As a reply to the world-wide demand for reform, one cannot imagine a more miscalculated and futile response than the lives, deeds, moral standards, and general corruption of the papal court. Only their benefactions to art, as patrons, and their concern for the preservation of ancient literature and sculpture—what was left of it after the barbarians, the Arabs, and the Christian emperors (e.g. Theodosius and Justinian) had destroyed whatever they could —this service to civilization should not be overlooked or forgotten. But it was no service to the Christian religion, save indirectly as an advantage to learning.

The belated Fifth Lateran Council (1512-17) accomplished little beyond the condemnation of the Council of Pisa which Louis XII of France had convoked in 1511 in opposition to Pope Julius II. The French army which undertook to invade Italy was repulsed by the loyal Swiss and Milanese and sent packing home across the Alps. But the new pope, Leo X, closed the Council with a bull, *Pastor aeternus gregem*,[10] condemning episcopalism. That was on December 19, 1516. On October 31, 1517, Martin Luther nailed his ninety-five theses to the door of the castle church in Wittenberg.

10. Denzinger, § 1445.

VI

Reformation and Counter Reformation:
1500-1700

Externally viewed, the Protestant Reformation was the greatest disaster that ever overtook the Roman Catholic Church. It might have been foreseen and, if foreseen, forestalled and avoided. Signs had not been wanting for two centuries and more in advance of the debacle. During the century immediately preceding the "revolution"—or "revolt," as some writers term it—these signs were greatly multiplied, indicating that things were seriously amiss and needed careful attention. The constant and repeated appeal for a general council; the blocking and silencing of councils when convened; the outcry against financial oppression and the scandal of two popes at once, or even three; the protests against the scandalous lives of the Renaissance hierarchy in Rome and Avignon; the political entanglement of the papacy with various powers, chiefly with France, to the detriment of its influence elsewhere; the rise of Gallicanism, and the sounding of similar notes of independence in other countries than France; the growth of nationality and the increasing strength of a territorial or local consciousness, distinct from and not always compatible with loyalty to the church as a whole, i.e. a *Landeskirchentum*, often with the king or the nobility on its side; the still unsolved problem of the relation of church and state, church and empire, pope and emperor; the spread of fanatical apocalyptic movements, a consequence of repressed reform, stifled freedom, and frustrated religious zeal, as significant in Europe in the fifteenth century as it had been in Palestine in the first—these were the signs which the church could ignore only at its peril; and it ignored them. No amount of external brilliance or glitter of artistic and literary distinction, under the patronage of a long series of fabulously wealthy and still pagan clerical Maecenases seated upon the papal throne, could disguise the fact that a revolution was in fact about to take place.

It is not our purpose to sketch the history of the Reformation, but only to note its salient features, their bearing upon the papacy, and the papal reaction to events. The total world-situation was a tripartite rivalry between three great powers, Spain, France, and England; both Italy and Germany were broken up into small duchies and city-states. Spain's hegemony, based on the wealth of the West Indies, Mexico, and Peru, enabled her to dictate the policies that were to control and guide Europe for a century. This was especially true after the alliance with the Hapsburgs combined Catholic Austria with Catholic Spain: both kingdoms were more devoted to the Catholic system than any of the northern powers, Germany, France, or England. The addition of Germany to this powerful coalition in 1519, when the throne of the Holy Roman Empire was added to those of Spain and Austria, under the now triple dominion of the young emperor Charles V (1519-56), immensely increased and unified this sovereign combination of Catholic powers. A loyal Catholic, Charles looked

upon his royal duty as including the restoration of the old
imperial authority, the support of the ancient church, and
the destruction of Islam, which after the fall of Constantinople in 1453 had steadily continued to move in the direction of western and northern Europe. By the end of the
fifteenth century it had crossed the Bosporus, and in 1529
it even threatened Vienna. The stages in this tidal advance
are clear. In 1521 Belgrade had been taken by Suleiman II;
in 1522 the Knights of St. John had abandoned Rhodes and
fallen back upon Malta; in 1526 Hungary had been overwhelmed. Though a futile gesture had been made by the
pope, threatening another crusade when Constantinople
fell in 1453, nothing had happened. If Europe, i.e. western
Christendom, was to be defended against the Turks, the
armies of the emperor must undertake the task.

On the brighter side was the still favorable economic
condition of the northern nations, especially Germany and
England, whose overseas trade and commerce and territorial expansion eclipsed that of France and rivaled that of
Spain. The British policy of expansion of trade and settlement was far more successful and more permanent than the
Spanish policy of conquest and loot. These economic and
political factors have often been ignored, but they were of
real importance for the spread of the Reformation when
once it got under way. All historians now recognize the
importance of this favorable set of factors which stood on
the side of the Reformation; even Roman Catholics recognize it—or, should we say, even Protestants! There are some
who deny the prosperity that eventually tipped the balance
in the North; but the data they cite are more relevant to
the century following, crowned by the awful devastation
of the Thirty Years War.

What Martin Luther undertook to do, when he nailed

his theses [1] to the church door at Wittenberg, was not to begin a religious revolution, or even a revolt against the papacy; he wished only to start a lively and fruitful debate on issues that the church was now facing, everywhere. But the fire he lighted led to a far bigger powder keg! Without intending it, without anticipating it, this simple, earnest, honest German Christian scholar found himself at the center, or rather at the head, of the most significant movement for church reform in all Christian history. The time had come, the hour had struck, the day of reckoning had arrived.

The main divisions of Protestantism, Lutheran (or Evangelical), Reformed (or Calvinist), Zwinglian, Anglican, and other—e.g. Anabaptist—were scarcely predictable in 1517, but were the result of personal leadership, experience, inherited beliefs, ideals, all stirred in the melting pot of a gigantic religious revolution. It was like the release of secret forces in an earthquake, or a "break" in the weather—unpredictable, and yet the result of known forces and tendencies. If all the factors had been known, and anyone had understood how to analyze or evaluate them, the result might perhaps have been foretold. But the "science of history" (if it is a science) had not reached that point of development in the sixteenth century. Nor has it reached it yet. Not even computing machines can help us! One thing seems clear: of all possible ways to face a religious revolution, or the threat of one, that of the sixteenth-century papacy was about the worst. Some of the popes undertook to suppress it. Others tried to ignore it, as if it were merely a local squabble among the German monks, something that could be kept "out of sight and out of mind." What was emerging, as Karl Heussi truly said, was

1. Bettenson, pp. 260-68; Mirbt, § 415.

a new form of Christianity.[2] Luther viewed "the gospel"
largely as Paul's interpretation represented it; not as the
faith reflected in the teaching of Jesus and in the earliest
gospels, but as that which is reflected in the Pauline letters
and in the Gospel of John. There was no such thing as a
historical understanding of Paul—or of the New Testament
—in the opening decades of the sixteenth century. Nor was
there in the later decades either, or in the Protestant or the
Catholic "orthodoxy" of the seventeenth and eighteenth
centuries. The result was a one-sided interpretation of the
gospel, as if it were centered in "justification by faith only,
apart from works of the Law," with its central text in
Romans 1.17, "He who through faith is righteous shall live"
(from Habakkuk 2.4), or, in the traditional translation,
"The just shall live by faith." The efforts of such a leader
as Melanchthon to steer a middle course, and to play fair
with the rest of the New Testament, resulted in a charge of
Pelagianism (or of Semi-Pelagianism) against him, "righteousness by works" and "reliance on the arm of flesh."
Although Melanchthon's influence is clear in the Augsburg
Confession (1530), it never characterized the central line
of development in Evangelical theology. Melanchthon was
accused, and is still, to this day, accused of "trimming" and
of trying to carry water on both shoulders, still "half a
Catholic." Others share the charge—Anglicans, for example, who endeavor to "keep a foot in each camp." So did
Erasmus, and others.

Of Calvin and his extreme version of Protestantism—
logical, legal, predestinarian, intolerant, vindictive, persecuting (there were many more victims than Servetus)—we
need not speak. The attitude of the popes, now fully
aroused to this type of Protestantism, was total opposition,

2. Heussi, p. 314.

without hope or expectation of any reconciliation, as some
had hoped for in the case of Luther. Even though strict
predestinarianism had been found here and there in earlier
theology, all the way back to Augustine, there had never
been so rigid a view, nor one tied to such a negative attitude toward much of Catholic doctrine and practice. (The
prevailing Augustinian theology which dominated the Western church down to the sixteenth century was, as Friedrich
Loofs maintained in his *Leitfaden*, really "Semi-Pelagianism"—accepted as if it were the full-blown Anti-Pelagianism
of the Carthaginian father's darker hours.) The persecution
of the (Calvinist) Huguenots, for example, though partly
explained by their political independence and intransigeance,
was the result of the isolation of Christians who, from the
Catholic viewpoint (and from that of the French cardinal
and the king), had cut themselves off from all communication with Catholic tradition and the central life in grace of
the one church of Christ.

In appraising Protestantism in its great main divisions, and
even in the stubborn minor sects which it produced, we must
never forget that all these people had once been Catholics.
The church should not have condemned them too severely,
for their views and their practices were the consequence
of their upbringing within Catholicism, and reflected the
church's success or failure to educate, to guide, to moderate,
in a word to Christianize nations originally barbarian. The
persecution of Protestants reflected the church's own pastoral and educational failure after ten centuries of patient effort, at first missionary, then parochial, at last of intensively
pastoral guidance of the northern peoples. The Reformation
was not only a disaster for Rome, but the evidence of a
catastrophic failure.

The reaction, and the beginning of the Counter Reformation, were not long in getting under way. Some of the popes, for example Paul III (1534-49), might delay and minimize the danger; the Curia, as a whole, might view the tempest as a transient summer storm; but the forces at work to check or counter the Protestant movement were not greatly delayed. The major strategy turned out to be three-fold: the founding of the Jesuit Order, the "Society of Jesus" (1540); the renewal of the Inquisition and its centering in Rome (1542); and the convening of the Council of Trent (1545-63). The Jesuits were so successful, so far-reaching, that, although Germany was over 60 per cent Protestant in 1570, it was only 30 per cent Protestant by 1600. Their efforts in other countries, often so intense and penetrating as to result in their banishment, was to be seen in the vacillation of various Protestant areas, groups, and rulers, and often their return to the Catholic fold. Their work for foreign missions, e.g. among the Muslims and in the Far East, was equally effective. In fact, one might almost say that the Jesuit Order saved the papacy, and that the history of the Roman Catholic Church since the sixteenth century is very largely the history of the Jesuits. The converse is also true: for they are really a military order, in spirit, demanding absolute obedience and identifying themselves without reserve with what they or their leaders conceived to be the true interests of the Catholic Church. If they were banished, repeatedly, even from "Catholic" countries, it was often the result of over-concentration upon the goal they had set themselves, viz. to defeat Protestantism and bring the nations of Europe back to full obedience to the church and full submission to its true spiritual head, who occupied the see of Peter.[3]

The Society of Jesus is one of the major historical manifestations of the Christian religion. We may disapprove its

3. Bettenson, pp. 364-7; Mirbt, §§ 430-33.

methods, even its motives, and its presuppositions, but first we must understand it. From the point of view of sixteenth-century Catholicism, there was nothing wrong, nothing even questionable, in either methods, motives, or presuppositions. It was the true *militia Christi* mustered for a great campaign, one far more significant and indispensable than any of the crusades into far-off Eastern lands had been. The unity, the holiness, even the existence of the church was now at stake, and the heroic men who had renounced all—even their own individual personality, freedom of will, purpose in life—to serve this great cause deserved all honor, all confidence. Their motto was *omnia ad maiorem Dei gloriam:* "Everything for the greater glory of God." The old Benedictines had deserved praise and gratitude; so had the Franciscans; so had many other orders. But now in an age of universal turmoil and danger, the orders that held the foremost rank were the Jesuits and the Dominicans, both of whom were committed to settle the crisis that confronted the Catholic Church everywhere on earth.

It was the worldly Pope Paul III (1534-49) who both reactivated the Inquisition and authorized the foundation of the Jesuit Order,[4] and who finally approved the emperor's demand for a general council. This council assembled at the mountain town of Trent, in the remotest corner of the German empire, nearest Italy, in December 1545. It was expected to continue, at most, for a year or two, like the older councils; but it ran on for eighteen years, until December 1563. Its chequered career reflected the continuing tension between the papacy and the emperor, and it was assembled, transferred, adjourned, closed, and reopened repeatedly. The emperor, Charles V (1519-56), wanted a practical solution of the pressing problem of

4. Mirbt, §§ 427-30.

religious and theological dissension and even separation within his realm, and an end to ecclesiastical parties. This requirement certainly presupposed or involved a compromise, with real concessions to the Protestants. His younger brother and successor, Ferdinand I (1556-64), continued this policy. But the Council was in reality firmly and almost unanimously anti-Protestant, from beginning to end. The only moderating force was the "episcopalism" reflected in some of its members, who opposed, for example, the formulation of the doctrine of papal infallibility—which finally won in 1870, more than three hundred years later.

The history of the Council [5] falls into three periods: (1) 1545-47 or -49, the most important of the three, which dealt with matters of doctrine, some of them (e.g. the Sources of the Church's Teaching) much the same as those presented for discussion and decision in 1962, at Vatican Council II. The outbreak of an epidemic in 1547 caused—or excused—the removal of the Council to Bologna, which was in papal territory, where it continued until 1549. There were only two sessions in Italy, after which Paul dismissed the assembly, and soon after died. (2) The new pope, Julius III (1550-55), urged by the emperor, reconvened the Council once more at Trent in 1551. The French Protestants held aloof, but certain German Evangelical representatives attended. These sessions, six in number, dealt chiefly with the sacraments. In 1552 the Council was adjourned for two years, as war seemed imminent (the advance of Moritz of Saxony), but the two years grew to ten. Meanwhile Pope Julius and two of his successors died. (3) The new pope, Pius IV (1559-65), who was the uncle of the saintly Charles Borromeo, reconvened the Council, again at Trent, and it concluded in two years (January

5. Bettenson, pp. 368-75; Denzinger, §§ 1500-1862; Mirbt, §§ 442-78.

1562–December 1563). This period was much more firmly dominated by the Jesuits, and real progress was made in dealing with current abuses, fiscal, liturgical, pastoral, and marital, including the lives and discipline of the clergy, reforms which were urged by the emperor. It also considered, but rejected, his proposal to permit the administration of the chalice (the communion cup) to the laity.

The achievements of the Council of Trent are obvious in all the later history of Roman Catholicism. The breach between the Roman Catholic Church and Protestantism was now complete. The dogmatic structure of Roman teaching was crystallized in the pattern provided by the Schoolmen, especially by St. Thomas Aquinas. Certain reforms were effected, but not all that were authorized were carried out. Among the reforms effected were the limitation set on the preaching of indulgences; an end to the admission of children to the monastic life, with vows which could not be cancelled in later life, even if the person involved turned out to have no monastic vocation; and the cancellation of papal "provisors" and "expectancies," whereby income from churches, monasteries, and their lands could accumulate and be held for some later use or appointment. Such formal publications as the Tridentine *Profession of Faith*,[6] designed to match and counteract the numerous Protestant "Confessions," with its oath of allegiance and submission to the pope (still in force); the *Roman Catechism*,[7] a manual of doctrine for pastors and teachers; the Roman Breviary and Missal; the two editions of the Latin Bible, the "Vulgate" or common version (1590, 1592); the *Index of Prohibited Books*[8]—all these bore the stamp of the explicitly

6. Bettenson, pp. 375-7; Denzinger, §§ 1862-70; Mirbt, § 480.
7. Mirbt, §§ 482-9.
8. Denzinger, §§ 1851-61; Mirbt, § 481.

Roman, papal point of view. Trent had not been a representative assembly of the Catholic church, but a council dominated by Rome, and its complete Romanization of the Western church was destined to be both a strength and a weakness to Catholicism during the following four hundred years. As some Roman Catholic scholars now hold, Trent transformed the church into a "fortress," which remained impregnable until "breached from within" by Pope John XXIII.

Not that Protestantism was much better off. The major divisions in Protestantism, and the incessant theological controversy and resulting schisms that took place, complicated by the wars of religion, the Dutch struggle for freedom from Spain, the English war with Spain, the Huguenot wars in France, followed by the catastrophic Thirty Years War on the continent, the victory of Protestantism in Sweden, which tipped the scale and saved Protestantism in the rest of Europe: all this long, grim, complicated tale was a story of conflict between the Reformation and the Counter Reformation (and also within the Reformation) during the sixteenth and seventeenth centuries. How hardly the peace was won and at what cost is clear from the long aftermath. As Nicholas Murray Butler used to say, "Europe has never yet recovered from the Thirty Years War." The struggles of central Europe during the nineteenth and twentieth centuries were a sequel to the carnage and devastation wrought during the first half of the seventeenth century. By 1570, it is estimated, 60 or 70 per cent of the population of Germany had become Evangelical. Protestants dominated the Reichstag, and it looked as if all Germany would soon be Protestant. But the efforts of the Jesuits, now at last backed by the Curia, made deep inroads among the Protestant population, reconverting many, both nobility and commoners, back to the faith of their fathers. As it turned out, the peak of Protestant success in Germany had been reached—and passed—about 1559 or 1560. A German "Congregation" (committee of cardinals) was now established in Rome, and a German college, supported by the Curia; papal nuncios were maintained in Vienna, Cologne, and Lucerne. By 1600, as has been seen, the whole outlook for Protestantism in Germany and German-speaking lands was completely altered. Bavaria and southern Germany were Catholic once more, and so were large areas in the North. Protestants no longer controlled the Reichstag. The attention paid to education by the Jesuits, and especially to the education of the nobility, made good returns—literally. In Austria, by 1598, Protestantism was virtually extinct.

Meanwhile the embattled Protestants continued to quarrel among themselves. Their greatest weakness was what Matthew Arnold described as the "dissidence of dissent," as true on the Continent as later in Puritan England. The dreary annals of Lutheran and Reformed orthodoxy and their internal struggles, the frozen dogmatism of the seventeenth century, the endless arid polemics of theologians, leave little to be proud of. With victory almost in their hands, and facing the prospect of total reformation "in head and members" throughout the length and breadth of Western Christendom, the wrangling theologians of central Europe threw away all chance of success. A thousand years of slow emergence from barbarism, under the paternalistic and authoritarian tutelage of the Roman hierarchy, had not, alas, schooled these ex-Catholics in tolerance and co-operation or led them to a profound enough emphasis on the genuinely religious issues involved in the contest. Scholasticism likewise contributed to their disputatious,

logical, purely formal approach to religion, to holy scripture, to the Christian faith, even to the miracle of the new
life in Christ. This dark period was one of terror, bloodshed, controversy, treason, betrayal, bigotry, and fanaticism. One might have thought the Christian religion was
coming to an end, so tragic was the scene. In fact, many
did so think, in the eighteenth century, the era of the
Aufklärung or Enlightenment.

The superior line of popes after the reforms at Trent
was in marked contrast to the "Renaissance" papacy preceding them. But their efforts at reform within the church,
and at expansion and conversion without, were not wholly
successful. They still relied on "the arm of flesh" and declined to become examples of a purely spiritual headship of
the Catholic Church. For example, Pius V (1566-72), an
ardent reformer, was also a persecuting fanatic, a Grand
Inquisitor, who renewed the famous bull of Urban V
(1364) which listed, condemned, and cursed all heretics by
name; this bull was to be read publicly in all churches
"once a year . . . when the people are mostly gathered for
worship." [9] He also undertook (in 1570) to dethrone Elizabeth I of England by pronouncing the ban against her,
intending thus to release all her subjects from their allegiance to the crown [10]—a solution by which Philip II of
Spain undertook to profit in 1588 when he launched his
"invincible armada" against England.

The next pope, Gregory XIII (1572-85), is chiefly remembered for his reform of the Julian calendar (omitting
October 5-14, 1582), a great social contribution with
which Protestants and the East were slow to agree—England adopted it in 1752, and the Eastern church not until

9. It was issued in final form by Urban VIII in 1627. See Mirbt, § 513.
10. Mirbt, § 491; Bettenson, pp. 338f.

1920. Sixtus V (1585-90) was the reformer of papal finance, and the fashioner of modern Rome (before Mussolini), destroying many ancient buildings and other landmarks in his effort to modernize the city. But he built St. Peter's dome, reorganized the Curia (with its present congregations), drove the bandits from the Papal States (they later returned), and supported France against Spain. (Britain was not the first or only power to practice the "balance of power.") His edition of the Vulgate (1590) was a waste of time and money. Two years later his successor, Clement VIII (1592-1605), produced a far more accurate and reliable text,[11] the one that has been in use ever since, i.e. until the great modern critical editions began to appear in the late nineteenth and early twentieth centuries.

On the whole the papacy during this dark time did not fare so ill. There was a deepening of the religious life in many areas, for example in Spain, where mysticism flourished. And in support of the confident appeal to tradition voiced at Trent, industrious research and collation of manuscripts produced new editions of the Church Fathers and new histories of the church. But as among the Protestants farther north, theology was chiefly dogmatic and polemical, though the Jesuits, with their strong emphasis on freedom of the will (as against determinism and predestinarianism), produced a whole literature on Moral Theology, especially Casuistry, law based on *cases*. Even the old and vexatious problem of the relations of church and state was handled by these scholars, for example by the saintly Robert Bellarmine.[12] (But his theory of an *indirect power* of the papacy over the empire, and over earthly rule in general, was rejected by Pope Sixtus V.) In defense of tradition, he

11. See Mirbt, § 498.
12. Mirbt, §§ 499-504.

scored a direct hit against the Protestant reliance on scripture: how can Protestants rely solely on the Bible when it is only tradition that tells us the Bible is authoritative? But the age was still theological, controversial, competitive, dogmatic, and opinionated. The dawn of modern science did not come until the seventeenth century. The ecclesiastical murder of Giordano Bruno in 1600, following the condemnation of his heliocentric and Copernican views, was the papal parallel to Calvin's murder of Servetus at Geneva in 1553. But the future belonged to both liberalism in religion and freedom in scientific research.

With the seventeenth century dawned a new day for both religion and science. Though with many setbacks, the slow emergence of a new spirit, more clearly to be seen at the end of the century than at its beginning, now began to be recognizable—not everywhere, but in certain bright areas. If it was the century of the Edict of Nantes and its revocation,[13] it was also the century of Hugo Grotius (1583-1645) and the Arminian "Remonstrance" (1610) against a rigid doctrine of predestination. It was also the century of the birth of modern science in astronomy, mathematics, history, biblical research, and other fields. The Roman Catholic Church distinguished itself by its enormous missionary efforts, though the popes were not a distinguished line from Paul V (1605-21) to Innocent XII (1691-1700). Once more the power and influence of the church rested upon alliances with earthly sovereigns—at first with Spain, still at the peak of its power and wealth, and later with France, which was steadily moving forward during this century. But even in Catholic countries the papacy was hindered and opposed. For example, in his quarrel with Venice, Paul V undertook to use the time-

13. Mirbt, § 536.

worn device of the ban and the interdict—with no result. The valiant Venetians went right on, regardless of the papal act, and continued to hold their services of worship, loyal to their doges and council, and appointing Fr. Paul Sarpi (1552-1623), who had written a history of the Council of Trent, to draw up their defense, a tract on the Interdict. He was an opponent of the temporal power of the popes. At the same time they banished the Jesuits; for the next fifty years not one Jesuit set foot in Venice. It was almost the last interdict ever pronounced by the papacy.

Paul's successor, Gregory XV (1621-3), was a friend of the Jesuits and made saints of Ignatius Loyola and Francis Xavier;[14] he also organized the Congregation of Propaganda,[15] i.e. the propagation of the faith. The next two popes were politically minded; but Alexander VII (1655-67) had the satisfaction of welcoming Queen Christina of Sweden into the Roman Catholic Church. She was the daughter of the great Protestant leader Gustavus Adolphus, whose army and valor had saved Protestantism in the Thirty Years War. She renounced the throne of Sweden in 1654, coming to live in Rome, and her body lies in St. Peter's.

It was also the century of revived "Gallicanism." The old struggle over the right to *regalia* (royal revenues) broke out again between Innocent XI (1676-89) and Louis XIV of France. This involved the right of the king to collect the income of a diocese or archdiocese during a vacancy in the episcopate. The French clergy supported the king in this struggle and in 1682 set forth *Four Propositions of the Gallican Clergy*,[16] principles of enduring sig-

14. Mirbt, § 512.
15. Mirbt, § 511.
16. Bettenson, pp. 380f; Mirbt, § 535; cf. Denzinger, §§ 2281-5; Cross, pp. 1387f ("Gallican Articles").

nificance in church-state relations down to and including
the First Vatican Council (in 1870). These were as follows: (1) Princes are independent of the spiritual power in
matters pertaining to temporalities. (2) The authority of
the pope in spiritual matters is limited by the decision of
a general council, as the Council of Constance had decreed.
(3) The papal power is limited by the law and customs of
the kingdom of France. (4) The judgment of the pope in
matters of faith is not infallible, unless it is sustained and
ratified by the general church. Eleven years later (1693)
the French clergy submitted to the pope, Innocent XII
(1691-1700), but the breach was not wholly healed and
the royal prerogative, the right to *regalia*, was no longer
questioned.

In general, elsewhere, the course of events ran smoothly
and true to form. Scientific research was checked and
opposed. In 1633 Galileo was compelled by the Inquisition
to retract his heliocentric views; but the great Maurist,
Jean Mabillon, published his magnificent researches in
church history; Jacques Bossuet, the bishop of Meaux,
preached his famous oratorical sermons; St. Francis de Sales
wrote his *Introduction to the Devout Life* and popularized
courtly mysticism (what Henri Brémond has called "devout
humanism"); and St. Vincent de Paul launched the widely
influential movement for charity and relief of the poor for
which he is famous. The Jesuits celebrated their Centennial
Jubilee in 1640, and they pursued their daring ventures
into "probabilism"—echoed, strangely, by the Anglican
bishop, Joseph Butler, a century later in his *Analogy of
Religion* (1736), "Probability is the very guide of life."
The meaning is that there are many cases where ethical
questions have no certain and unquestionable solution, and
only probability can guide us. What is probably the right

course is the one where more good than evil is likely to
result from its choice and pursuit. The dilemmas of modern
man provide ample illustration of this situation, whether
or not the solution is still described as "probabilism." The
Jansenist movement, named for Cornelis Jansen (1585-
1638), the Dutch divine who maintained the rigid teaching
of St. Augustine against the Jesuit theologians; the Port
Royalists and Blaise Pascal (1623-62) who shared Jansen's
views; the mystic Miguel de Molinos (1640-96), the
founder of Quietism; Madame Jeanne Marie Bouvier de la
Motte-Guyon (1648-1717), another Quietist; and Abp.
François Fénelon of Cambrai, a semi-Quietist—these all
belong to this wonderful seventeenth century.

But in England and Scotland the course of events was
exciting and dangerous, from James I (1603-49; he was
James VI of Scotland) to William and Mary (1689-1702)
and Queen Anne (1702-14): it was the era of the English
Civil War; of the execution of Charles I (1649); the period
of the Commonwealth (1649-60) of which Oliver Crom-
well was "Protector" (1653-8); of the Restoration and the
final settlement, the "glorious revolution" of 1688; the Act
of Toleration (1689), and the end of all threat of a Roman
Catholic conquest with a restoration of the Roman type of
Catholicism. Despite the activity of the "Roman mission"
and the efforts of the Jesuits, despite the threat of invasion
from Scotland or Ireland—or the Continent—and despite
the rise of "Independency" and a powerful Puritan Non-
conformity, the Church of England continued on a fairly
even keel, and the settlement of 1688 (the centenary of
the Armada!) came as a blessing to all parties, even to the
"English Catholics." Nevertheless, the Stuarts, meanwhile,
were planning a powerful return in force, which the later
pitiful adventures of "Bonnie Prince Charlie," the events

of "the '15" and "the '45" only showed up for what they were: futile, groundless, insubstantial daydreams. The tomb of the Stuarts in St. Peter's is the last sad record of a deeply misguided loyalty and a totally impractical enthusiasm.

But for the English-speaking world, the quiet studies of a group of philosophical theologians, the "Cambridge Platonists," provided the bright promise of a better day. Far from the strife of tongues, silent amid the roaring collision and controversy of the mid-seventeenth century, they pursued their researches and continued to advocate the use of reason, "the divine governor of man's life," but declining to set Reason and Spirit in opposition—how could Platonists ever do so? As their leader, Benjamin Whichcote (1609-83), insisted, "spiritual is most rational." Their view of the gospel and the Christian teaching as a whole was quite different from the views prevailing in their time: the gospel sets forth a way of life, not a system of dogma to be analyzed and expounded logically and defended against all comers. They were as clearly distinguished from Puritanism as from Catholicism, and their emphasis upon the unchanging ethical element in religion prepared the way for the moral philosophy of their own and the following century. Their contribution is still to be seen in areas (especially in Anglicanism and in Christian liberalism) where concern is felt for things deeper than formal dogmatics or apologetics, ritual or canon law.

Thus "through good report and evil report" the papacy muddled on for another century and more. New forces were gathering, all unknown, and a crisis almost matching that of the sixteenth century was steadily advancing over the dim horizon of the future. The course of history was leading to a political revolution in France destined to shake the whole of Europe and to have repercussions that have lasted to this day. Only "the things that cannot be shaken" (cf. Heb. 12.26-8) were to stand fast in this time of trial; and all institutions, religious and secular, all customs, presuppositions, superstitions, and idle fancies, however ancient and venerable, were soon to be tested by a new criterion of reality and truth, and of usefulness to mankind, one which had never before been so radically, so drastically, so ruthlessly applied.

VII

Since 1700

It is the cherished conviction of most conservatives that
institutions do not change, that they may remain the same
for centuries and, if well and truly founded, will necessarily remain unchanged, perhaps for ever. But modern
history has proved this view illusory.

> Time goes, you say? Ah no!
> Alas, Time stays, *we* go.

Austin Dobson's famous lines—it is a common theme of his:
"All passes"—are as true of institutions as of individuals.
Thrones and empires, constitutions and systems of law,
philosophies and theologies, even religions alter with the
changing ages. In the midst of a world of change ("the
world *is* change," as Marcus Aurelius wrote), institutions
must change in order to maintain, not their position but
their very existence. As the French adage puts it, things
must constantly change in order to remain the same. In a
relativistic universe, where "nothing continueth in one
stay," it cannot be otherwise. No star in the heavens, no
planet in its wheeling course through space, ever occupies

precisely the same position twice, for the whole system is in constant motion, though

> Whither vainer sounds than whence
> For word with such wayfarers.

Like the horse in the treadmill, only constant "progress" enables institutions to stay where they are!

Yet there is an element of real progress in all this change. Only those deny it today who seem unaware of the history of our civilization. And in the church there has been progress too. The Christian church in the West is not now, and has not been since the seventeenth century, what it was before then. And yet it is still recognizably the Christian church. Also it is a better church, a more realistic institution, a more effective instrument for divine uses than it was in earlier times. The old fanaticism and superstition, the old intolerance and compulsion, the old ostracism and persecution have been left behind, and they are gradually disappearing even in the backward regions of the earth. Or, if they are not actually disappearing, they are now recognized for what they are, shameful and disgraceful, and incompatible with genuine humanity and civilization. That is the next step to repudiation. The idea of compelling anyone to accept the Christian faith, or to profess it in legally formulated specific theological terms, has all but disappeared in Christian countries. Such a faith, or its profession, is futile and valueless. The idea of a church appointed by God to rule the nations and anoint or dethrone kings, able to pronounce a ban upon the disobedient or an interdict upon whole populations, thus creating social chaos in order to enforce the "spiritual" authority of the church's head—such an idea is now so antiquated that it would only provoke ridicule if it were to be advocated. But the release of Western society from this incubus upon its political freedom was purchased at a high price, in the sixteenth and seventeenth centuries. Instead of a religious motivation of political life, we now have an increasing "separation of church and state" that leaves our political institutions and procedures at the mercy of secularism, materialism, commercial greed, brute force, and bitter prejudice. Even the Christian in politics cannot appeal to Christian principles, or the Jew to Jewish principles; instead, he must base his appeals and arguments upon motives as barefaced and primitive as those that reign in countries dedicated to atheism. We have not yet lived out the consequences of the seventeenth-century secularization of political and social life, of which the eighteenth-century Revolution in France and its later repercussions in Germany and elsewhere were the inevitable consequence. The real revolution began in the realm of ideas, as always. Guns and bombs and guillotines came after.

Not only was Protestantism affected by the great turn of the tide in the eighteenth century; it also affected Catholicism, and, as always, both for worse and for better. The evil results of the new freedom were seen in the futile efforts to oppose and prevent it, especially by appeal to force. The good results were the final triumph of the principles of liberty and freedom of assembly, of speech, of the press, and of religious belief. Nowadays, Catholicism enjoys these rights and privileges fully as much as do Protestantism and secularism and every other type of thought or belief.

The crumbling of the ancient dikes took place in the period known as the *Aufklärung* or Enlightenment. It began in Holland about 1650 and in England about 1700. Much of the religious and theological or philosophical

writing of the time was negative, in an effort to clear away
useless or meaningless accretions and get back to the pure
quintessence of religion, its primitive form, freed from the
later entanglements of creeds, organizations, and priestly
professionalism or priestcraft. Some of the speculation was
childish, for example the theory of Lord Herbert of Cher-
bury (1581-1648) that the "common notions" of all men,
which were born within them, were five in number and
explained all later religious developments: (1) there is one
God; (2) he must be worshiped; (3) this worship consists
chiefly in virtue and piety; (4) man must repent of his sins,
and avoid them; (5) God rewards virtue and punishes sin,
both in this world and the next.[1] Much of this sounds like
ancient Stoicism. Far more bizarre was the somewhat later
theory of John Toland (1670-1722), in *Christianity Not
Mysterious* (1696), according to which this original, purely
rational religion was perverted by three influences, Judaism,
the Greek mysteries, and Platonic philosophy. Absurd as
were these views, and even monstrous (e.g. the political
views of Thomas Hobbes, 1588-1679), the *Aufklärung*
with its hard rationality and sharp debates was an essential
and unavoidable stage in the development of modern
thought, modern freedom, modern convictions.

On the Continent, the movement known as Pietism and
the pendulum-swing away from it to Rationalism and Nat-
uralism, and the rise of German Idealism in philosophy—
this whole sweeping, turbulent, irresistible tide of thought
and feeling that preceded the French Revolution and the
era of Napoleon and was reflected in the far corners of the
Western world, even in distant North America, was as
inevitable as springtime or daybreak. Out of it came, for

1. Cf. the views of other Deists and Latitudinarians in Bettenson, pp.
439-44; Cross, p. 385 ("Deism").

good or ill, what we now look upon as our world, this
modern and very different society we endure, tolerate, or
rejoice in. How fared the Roman Catholic Church, and
especially the papacy, during this tumultuous era of change?

There were eight popes from Clement XI (1700-1721)
to Pius VI (1775-99), and they exactly filled out the eighteenth century. The period opened with a setback—as often
happens in papal history, with its constant oscillation or
pendulum motion of alternating strength and weakness.
The efforts at political coercion all failed: for example,
Clement's quarrel with the emperor Joseph I and with
Victor Amadeus II of Savoy; Benedict XIII's attempt to
bring the Swiss canton of Lucerne into line; Benedict XIV's
appeal to external force in dealing with foreign powers;
the attempts to compel Protestants to return to Catholicism,
especially Protestant minorities in Catholic countries—following the earlier brief but ineffectual efforts of Leibniz,
Bossuet, and others to reunite Protestantism and Catholicism, efforts that merely demonstrated the futility of all
such attempts under the conditions of that time and with
the totally divergent outlooks of the two groups. The inner
life, the spiritual leadership, the breadth and comprehension, the charity and good will of the central officers of the
church, the popes and the Curia, were simply not equal to
the task. Furthermore, the campaign buckled for lack of
support as well as for lack of leadership.

The Jesuits also suffered great setbacks. In Portuguese
Paraguay, an armed Indian revolt, engineered, it was said,
by the Order, collapsed and led to their expulsion not only
from Paraguay but from Portugal itself and all its other
colonies. In France, the bankruptcy of a Jesuit trading post
in Martinique led Parlement to demand that the creditors
be repaid in full, and to forbid the Order to engage in

secular business, as contrary to law and a danger to the
state. In spite of Louis XV's effort to reform, and thus save,
the Order, he was compelled by popular protests to banish
it from France. This action was followed by the courts of
Spain, Naples, and Parma. For the Jesuits, it was their
darkest hour. Finally, on July 21, 1773, Pope Clement XIV,
appealing to divine inspiration (see his letter, *Dominus ac
Redemptor noster* [2]), pronounced the permanent dissolution of the Jesuit Order. Curiously, it was only Frederick II
of Prussia and Catherine II of Russia who gave them safe
refuge.

The dissolution and banishment of the Jesuits, coupled
with the well-known debasement of the French court,
were no preparation for the tornado of revolution that
followed in 1789. Down went the *ancien régime*, and with
it the Gallican church. Bitter hatred of religion, church,
clericalism, church taxes, church dogma, even of Christian
ethics, prevailed under the Terror. When the Revolution
ended, the church's property had been confiscated by the
state, monasteries and religious orders had been dissolved,
the clergy made subject to choice by the people (40,000 of
them objected, refused to taken an oath of allegiance to the
Constitution, and were banished), two thousand churches
were devastated and robbed of their artistic treasures. The
religious freedom that was guaranteed in the end (1795)
was that of a non-religious state.

In Rome, Pius VI endeavored at first to ride out the
storm; but he soon became involved in difficulties with the
new government and prepared for war. The result of this
appeal to arms was the Treaty of Tolentino (1797), according to which General Napoleon Bonaparte extracted thirty
million livres from the pope and the cession of a large part

2. Mirbt, § 548.

of the Papal States. In 1798 the French government set up
the Roman Republic and still further harrassed the temporal power of the papacy. Pius was seized and taken as a
prisoner to France, where he died the following year. However, his successor, Pius VII (1800-1823), under the protection of the Austrians, the English, the Russians, and the
Turks, was able to enter the Vatican Palace. The Roman
Republic was abolished, and the Papal States restored.

The ups and downs of historical change next brought
about another curious reverse. Napoleon's military despot-
ism led directly to a renewed position of influence for the
church in France. Convinced that he could not fight the
church, and realizing its value as an unpaid police force,
the Catholic Church was restored by the Concordat of
1801. Elsewhere, the story was different. In Germany, both
the old German Empire, i.e. "the Holy Roman Empire of
the German Nation," was abolished, in 1806, and the Catholic Church was secularized. What lay in store for Great
Britain, once Napoleon succeeded in crossing the Channel,
was obvious to the whole world. But he did not cross!
In 1809 Pope Pius was arrested and deported to France.

The menace of Napoleon Bonaparte was eventually destroyed, and in 1815 the nations of Europe set about restoring what was left after his career of armed murder and
destruction had run its course. This was naturally accompanied by a return swing of religious feeling, which in
some countries swept away much of the work of the
Aufklärung. The shrewd good sense of the nineteenth-
century popes took full advantage of this change. Even the
strange and exciting movement we know as Romanticism
was used to advantage—it surrounded the ancient church
with an aura of golden sunshine, it created a world of
fantasy and imagination that fostered a renewal of piety

and devotion. In fact, the nineteenth-century papacy won
back almost all that had been lost since the end of the
fourteenth century, in purely religious and intellectual con-
cerns as also in political and material. The same forces that
produced Anglo-Catholicism in England were also effective on the Continent. Men idealized—and idolized—the
"ages of faith," and tried to get behind the negative, critical,
dissolving ethos that had prevailed ever since those ages had
come to an end. It was of course an attitude fatal to contact
with those in the modern world who believed in the separation of the church from worldly affairs. From the 1840's
onward, the movement toward the complete secularization
of politics, economics, education, public welfare, scientific
research, and philosophy, gained increasing momentum.
The rise of Socialism was a good example of the new substitute for church and religion. Despite the religious crisis
of the century and the slow advance of Protestantism out
of its traditional conservatism to a new and more liberal
position, both theologically and politically, the eventual
awakening of the non-Catholic Christian groups was certain. The political successes of the papacy were matched
in Protestantism by other modes of extending influence.
On the part of both Protestants and Catholics, there was a
wholly unexampled growth of foreign missions, active
throughout the entire non-Christian world.

The fall of Napoleon marked a turn in the tide for the
papacy: it was the day of liberation. Pius VII returned to
Rome in May 1814. The Congress of Vienna restored the
Papal States[3] and gave back to the pope the power to
enforce the prohibition of ideas, customs, movements based
on the *Aufklärung* or the French Revolution. The convents
were reopened, schools were re-established, and offices of

3. Mirbt, § 565.

state once held by the clergy were restored. The three following popes, Leo XII (1823-9), Pius VIII (1829-30),
Gregory XVI (1831-46), pursued a similar policy. The
Index was revived and revised; all anti-Catholic secret societies, e.g. the Free Masons, were condemned; Bible societies
(including Catholic Bible societies) were described as a
"pest"; and the education of the clergy was shifted from
universities, which were now tainted with ideas derived
from the Enlightenment, to orthodox seminaries, steeped
in Tridentine theology. Most important of all, Pope Pius
VII had lost no time in restoring (August 7, 1814) the
Jesuit Order to its former position of influence and responsibility.[4] It had been more than forty years "in the wilder-
ness" since the Order was dissolved by Clement XIV. The
speed with which the Order recovered its lost ground and
advanced into new fields, growing steadily in numbers and
influence, is one of the most phenomenal demonstrations of
vitality in all religious history.

The papacy likewise began a new era. By the end of
the reign of Pius VII, in 1823, the alliances and concordats
with various European states had secured once more the
legal position of the Roman Catholic Church in most places
where it had formerly been enjoyed. This set the church
free once more to promote its religious and educational
interests, in Protestant as well as in Catholic areas. Even the
reverses in later decades, such as the July Revolution of
1830 and the later one in February 1848, were useful. The
ball was caught on the rebound, and the surge of popular
revulsion against terrorism, anarchy, barricades, and tyranny served in the end to strengthen the church and its
influence.

The extraordinary reign of Pius IX (1846-78, almost a

4. Mirbt, § 564.

third of a century), was a long period of change and advance for the Roman Catholic Church. Beginning as a liberal and reformer, he became an avowed enemy of modern "progress" as a result of the European revolution of 1848, which toppled papal dominion in Italy and expelled the Jesuits once more. The pope fled southward along the coast to Gaeta and remained there in exile for two years, until the French and Austrian troops put down the revolution in Rome. This cured him. Returning to the city in 1850 he was ever after an out-and-out foe of liberalism. Pius's restoration was also the restoration of the Jesuits, who from now on took over the real leadership of the Roman Church. Even the rise of the Italian Risorgimento, with the anticlerical government of Piedmont at its head, did not stay the might of the increasingly powerful papacy, the Jesuit Order, and the Curia. In the very thick and press of the rising movement, and contrary to the wishes of many Catholic theologians, the pope proceeded, in the Bull *Ineffabilis Deus* (December 8, 1854),[5] to define the dogma of the Immaculate Conception of the Blessed Virgin Mary, and to decree it as a doctrine requiring acceptance by all Catholics. Ten years later, to the day, he issued the Encyclical *Quanta cura*[6] and the *Syllabus*[7] naming and condemning eighty errors found in modern thought, religious, scientific, political, and economic. Some of these were identified as "Americanism," by which he did not mean loyalty to American ideals in politics or "the American way of life" (some aspects of which he might well have condemned), but the growing practice—already rejected by the bishops— of making laymen responsible for the temporal affairs and

5. Denzinger, §§ 2800-2804; Mirbt, § 596.
6. Denzinger, §§ 2890-96.
7. Denzinger, §§ 2901-80; Mirbt, § 602.

property of the church, as the Wardens and Vestrymen are responsible for the material "fabric" in Episcopalian parishes. The whole *Syllabus*, which was collected from earlier statements of Pope Pius, reflects the influence of the Jesuits and their quondam emphasis on Scholastic and Tridentine theology.

The greatest achievement of Pope Pius IX was the convening of the First Vatican Council [8] in 1869, even though the triumph was brief. The Franco-Prussian war now threatening, the French troops left Rome. General Cadorna and the new Italian army moved in, and the Council had to be adjourned *sine die* on October 20, 1870. Only two of the subjects (*schemata*, draft decrees) proposed for consideration had been dealt with: *On the Catholic Faith* and *On the Church*. Over 80 per cent of the nearly seven hundred Council fathers were Italians, many of them Romans, i.e. residents of Rome, directly under the pope. In spite of the opposition of bishops from Germany, Austria, France, and the United States, after months of debate and many speeches of unlimited length, and after many of the objecting minority had gone home, the constitution *Pastor Aeternus* was passed on July 18, 1870—by a vote of 533 to 2.[9] It decreed that the pope has complete and immediate jurisdiction over the whole church, and that when he speaks *ex cathedra* (i.e. formally, "from the throne") on any subject relating to faith or morals his statement is

8. Denzinger §§ 3000-3075; Mirbt, §§ 605-6.

9. Denzinger, §§ 3050-75; Mirbt, § 606. See Dom Cuthbert Butler, *The Vatican Council*, new ed., Fontana Books, 1962, pp. 265-9; see also J. B. Bury, *History of the Papacy in the Nineteenth Century*, ed. Frederick C. Grant, New York, 1964.

On July 13 the vote had been 451 to 88, with 62 voting *placet juxta modum* ("with reservations"). Obviously many abstained or were absent on July 18. See Butler, p. 400.

infallible. In theory, this power rests upon the words of Christ to St. Peter in Matthew 16.18f. The pope's infallible decree needs no confirmation by church or council, but is *ex sese* final and irreformable. Just how this attribution of authority could be made *by* a council was not explained; presumably it was by acknowledgment.

Needless to say, neither Pius IX nor any later pope has chosen to exercise this authority with any degree of frequency, even in the midst of most pressing problems of faith and morals. The dramatic anticlimax of the Council was Victor Emmanuel II's occupation of Rome, the fall of the Papal States (September 20, 1870), and the decision of the people of Rome to join the Kingdom of Italy (by a vote of 133,000 to 1500). In spite of the pope's ban, King Victor Emmanuel took over his residence in the Quirinal Palace. And despite the offer of sovereign rank and unhindered diplomatic exit and access to the Vatican Palace, the St. John Lateran basilica, and the Villa Castel Gandolfo, together with a yearly income of 3,225,000 lire, Pius rejected the whole proposal and shut himself up in the Vatican. Here, until 1929, he and each of his successors remained "the prisoner of the Vatican."

The new definition of papal infallibility was accepted by all Roman Catholic bishops, even by those who had protested against it. A small group of Roman Catholics in Holland and Germany seceded and formed the Old Catholic Church, which still survives and flourishes, with no outstanding differences between them and the Roman Catholic Church except for their rejection of the Infallibility Decree.[10] They were represented by observers at the Second Vatican Council, in 1962-64. Stronger opposition came from Prince Bismarck, premier of the new German

10. Mirbt, §§ 732-5, esp. 734.

Empire, who unleashed a *Kulturkampf* (a cultural campaign aimed at control of education) against the Roman
Catholic Church in 1872-9. But it was only a passing
episode. Bismarck's political motives were all too obvious.
Again the church triumphed and, in doing so, won praise
from its enemies.

This was the situation when Pope Leo XIII (1878-1903)
began his reign. His great gifts as an ecclesiastical statesman and organizer were evident throughout his long term
of office. Though adhering closely to the views of his predecessors, he tried to mollify the opposition and in some
measure make friends with Protestants. He encouraged the
laity to study the Bible; he created a well-chosen hierarchy;
he reached out to influence non-Catholics and whole cultural groups, even non-Christian; he dealt boldly and con-
structively with social questions, especially in his famous
encyclical *Rerum novarum* (1891) [11]; and he undertook to
make the theology of St. Thomas Aquinas normative for
the whole church.[12] He was in fact one of the greatest
statesmen ever to occupy the papal throne—one of perhaps
a half-dozen of the very highest in rank and in influence
upon the whole Christian world. But he did not rule single-
handed. The Curia was active and sometimes opposed his
plans and wishes. It is said, for example, that the decision
against the validity of Anglican Orders (September 13,
1896) was a defeat for the pope, who favored their recognition.[13] But the decision was in harmony with his general
view on interchurch relations.

Leo's successor, Pope Pius X (1904-14), was a devout
and godly Christian who undertook to "restore all things

11. Denzinger, §§ 3265-71.
12. Denzinger, §§ 3135; Mirbt, § 616.
13. Denzinger, §§ 3315-19; Mirbt, § 635.

in Christ" (*omnia instaurare in Christo*). The decline of the church in France and the outbreak of World War I in 1914 were a cause of great pain and grief to his simple, devout spirit. The Modernist movement was also a sore wound, though it was suppressed in 1907 with a new syllabus, *Lamentabili*,[14] and the encyclical *Pascendi dominici gregis*.[15] "Modernism" was denounced as the sum of all heresies and errors in faith. The stubborn ultra-conservatism of this pious but reactionary leader would have pleased Pius IX and many of his predecessors. The victory over the minority was sealed by the so-called Anti-Modernist Oath,[16] required of all professors, confessors, preachers, official representatives of the church, and still others. A Pontifical Biblical Commission was organized [17] (1911) to defend the faith against modern views of the Bible, e.g. the Two Source Theory of the Synoptic Gospels. The motive was obviously fear of the unknown: the reactionaries neither knew nor understood the grounds upon which modern biblical views are based, and they declined to take the trouble to find out. Later popes have modified this unfortunate stand, but it is still hard to find Roman Catholic scholars who are really free to deal with biblical problems, especially in the New Testament, and with questions relating to Christian origins, unfettered by prior dogmatic assumptions.

The next pope, Benedict XV (1914-22), had the difficult task of maintaining contact with both sides during World War I and after.[18] But though not a party to the making

14. Denzinger, §§ 3401-66; Mirbt, § 652.
15. Denzinger, §§ 3475-3500; Mirbt, § 653.
16. Denzinger, §§ 3537-50; Mirbt, §§ 657-8.
17. Denzinger, §§ 3561-7.
18. Mirbt, §§ 659-63.

of the peace, nor represented there, the moral authority of
the pope rose steadily during the war and during the years
that followed. Fresh efforts were made to form alliances
or agreements with various nations, and papal nuncios were
sent to many of the leading European cities. One of his
great achievements was the new edition of the *Codex Iuris
Canonici* (1918), the body of Roman Catholic church law
in 2414 Canons dealing with internal regulations such as
the administration of the sacraments, or the church law
governing marriage, but not with such delicate or dangerous matters as the relations between church and state. To
say the least, these relations varied in different countries,
and no general legislation could be devised to cover every
contingency.

Pius XI (1922-39) ruled during the dull period between
the two world wars, the *Zwischen den Zeiten* ("Between
Times") which did so much to depress Protestant theology.
Pius's efforts to stay the advance of both Communism and
National Socialism (in both Germany and Italy) were
unsuccessful: the madness that had seized the followers of
Benito Mussolini and Adolf Hitler was beyond the wisdom
of even the wisest to heal.

His successor, Pius XII (1939-58) bore the full brunt of
the Fascist-Nazi attack upon the church and the Christian
religion, as well as upon Judaism, the Western allies, and
Russia. A recent German play, *Der Stellvertreter* ("The
Deputy" or "The Substitute") by Rolf Hochhuth, has
described the pope as timid in his championship of the
persecuted and martyred Jews. But those who remember
the time recall the words of Pope Pius XI, "We Christians
are also Jews," and Pope Pius XII's efforts to protect the
Jews in Rome. Whether or not he endeavored to protect

those in Germany and elsewhere is still debated; or whether he tried and failed. In 1939 he had warned Hitler against going to war. Once the war was on, he followed his predecessor's policy in maintaining contact with both sides—there were millions of Catholics on both sides. The respect shown the Vatican and the churches in Rome by the contending armies was largely a token of respect for the pope. At least this is what was and still is being said; though one wonders if it was not really reverence for the holy places of all Christendom by friends and foes alike. The destruction of St. Peter's, for example, would have brought down upon either side the undying emnity not only of the foe but of their own people. (The shameful destruction of the ancient Benedictine abbey at Monte Cassino, it is said, was a direct result of its use by the Nazis as a fortification or observation post.) The brave efforts of individual Catholics in Germany, France, Switzerland, Belgium and Holland—and even in Italy—to shield and save the Jews did more to commend the Roman Catholic faith to the world in general than mountains of propaganda and special pleading. Almost the whole world, including the non-Christian nations, now for the first time in modern history have only respect and reverence for those who dared to face mad tyrants and human butchers and demand justice for the oppressed. Like the Messiah in Psalm 72, it was the pope's office to "defend the cause of the poor . . . and give deliverance to the needy." That he did not succeed is no evidence that he did not try. Did anyone else try?

Even while the war continued, this valiant, austere, reserved scholar-pope found time to encourage biblical studies, and to give a fresh breath of life to religious scholarship, which still languished under the repressive Anti-Modernist decrees. His famous encyclical, *Divino afflante*

Spiritu (September 30, 1943),[19] marked the dawn of a new day in Roman Catholic biblical research.

When Pope John XXIII succeeded Pius XII in 1958 he inherited a great accumulation of good will which had been gathering ever since the days of Leo XIII. All the world knows how he increased this precious heritage. His charitable spirit; his interest in the poor and needy; his affectionate warmth and generous feeling toward the "separated brethren," as he preferred to call them, in the East and the North, in the West and elsewhere; his unflagging courage and optimism; his deeply Christian hope for better things, including peace among the nations and reconciliation (he would not say "submission") among the churches; his appeal for a real "updating" of the Roman Catholic Church, an *aggiornamento* to open the windows wide and let the fresh air of heaven sweep through the church—all these qualities won for him, and for the Roman Catholic Church throughout the world, the affectionate good will and renewed confidence of countless human beings, Christian and non-Christian, even in the far corners of the earth. He seemed to come as God's particular gift to this generation, in a world grown dark with trouble and alarm.

Pope John died on June 3, 1963, after a heroic battle with a malady from which he had suffered for many years. But the brevity of his reign is no measure of the influence he exerted and has left behind him. The Second Vatican Council, which he convoked in 1962, has been the bright promise of a realization of his aims and ideals for the Roman Catholic Church and for the whole of Christendom. The successor who was chosen to walk in his steps, Pope Paul VI, has begun his career with a high heart and rich promise of success. It is impossible that the church can slip back

19. Denzinger, §§ 3825-31.

into its old nineteenth-century position, let alone that of earlier centuries. It is the most alive institution in the world, albeit the oldest; and it is the most promising. Its program is the most likely to succeed, if properly supported. In it lies a hope for mankind that no earthly government or organization hitherto has even attempted to fulfill. The hope of a united Christendom, at long last, is a dream of world service which no world empire has ever aspired to realize—not even the aspirations of Constantine, or those of the mediaeval would-be world emperors in the West, could match it.

The purpose of this brief outline of the history of the papacy since the fourth century has been to show its positive contributions to religion and society, while acknowledging its defects and failures when they were apparent and did damage to the church or to the world. The sketch began with the fifth century for a good reason: it was the century in which papal influence began to be felt widely and to bear fruit politically and socially. At the least, it is clear that the papacy has been a valuable institution, without which Europe and America might still be barbarian— or, must we say, far more barbarian than they still are. As a spiritual institution, that and nothing more, without lands or armies, this high office could be still more influential throughout the world, and might bring about the world peace and international justice, the inter-racial harmony, good will and brotherhood for which men and women in all nations long and pray. A completely disinterested, devoted, consecrated papacy, exercising a leadership worthy of its highest titles, "Servant of the servants of God" and "Christ's representative (Vicar) on earth," would be a blessing beyond compare and might indeed bring the whole

world "not far from the Kingdom of God." For all its
failings in the past, for all its blunders and mistakes, and the
folly of a few selfish, self-seeking, or cowardly men, the
general course and aim of the institution has been forward
and upward. Far from discarding it, or disregarding it, and
in spite of the false claims often made for it and the flimsy
exegesis its apologists have too often employed, the papacy
is one of the most priceless elements in the Christian heritage. Reformed and restored to a pristine state in which,
among the church's leaders, it should be once more first
among equals, *primus inter pares*, rather than a monarchical
sovereignty, the papacy might very well become the acknowledged leader, guide, and chief of the whole Christian
church, and the greatest influence for good in all the world.
The question is still *Quo vadis*—"Whither goest thou?" It is
to more and greater influence for good, let us hope.

VIII

The Origin of the Papacy

What then is the papacy? and how does it provide a main obstacle to Christian reunion between Protestantism and Catholicism? Quite clearly, the papacy has been a blessing to many generations in the past, and may still prove a great advantage to world peace and welfare in the future. At present it is under fire, chiefly for its failure to prevent the extermination of six million Jews by the German Nazis in World War II—a question of responsibility which is still *sub judice*. But the obstacle does not consist in the papal principle, i.e. the principle of single and sole leadership of the whole of Christendom, or of sovereignty over the whole Christian church; nor does it consist even in the papal primacy, which could be explained satisfactorily and even made desirable to a divided and distracted modern world, in which the primacy might conceivably do much to arrest the present decline of civilization and public order throughout the whole world. But it is the additional, ancillary, inferential doctrines, beliefs, and practices that have grown up about the papacy, like vines on a tree, that form the great hindrance: infallibility, autocracy (especially in

the official representatives of the papacy, viz. the Roman
Curia), obsolete customs and "red tape," and the whole
assumption or presupposition of a divine authorization of
the papal claims, reflected both in historical documents and
in the consistent—and really unnecessary—misinterpretation
of biblical passages in a superficial, unnatural, and purely
juridical way.

What then is the papacy, if it is the chief obstacle to
Christian reunion? How did it originate, and how are other
doctrines and practices so attached to it that they depend
upon it, and not it upon them? And how can the conception of the papal primacy be altered (if that is possible),
without loss to Roman Catholicism, and to the advantage
of the whole Church of Christ, and yet retain its central
and organic connection with the rest of Christian belief
and practice? Or is it unalterable, so that change would
only result in collapse—like the great tree about which the
king's house was built in Norse and Teutonic legend, a tree
that supported the roof and sheltered the king's bed, and
symbolized the Tree of Life, the world tree Yggdrasill?
These are the questions that now confront us. They are
fundamental to the whole program and problem of reunion.

The traditional and historic theological discussions of
Roman Catholic–Protestant–Orthodox and Anglican differences no longer fit the case, e.g. the famous letter to the
Countess of Peterborough written by Bishop John Cosin of
Durham (1594-1672) [1] in which are listed the agreements
and disagreements between Anglicanism and Rome; and so
also many of the irenic (and certainly the polemical) books
of long ago are no longer applicable. The only theology
likely to be of any value today is rooted in the actual,
present-day spiritual and moral life of men and women; it

1. Bettenson, pp. 427-32. See Cross, p. 346 ("Cosin, John").

and it alone corresponds to and interprets reality as we understand it today—even in the small measure that we really do understand it. Appeals to ancient texts are more or less interesting, but they do not prove enough in this generation. They are like appeals to genealogy or to ancient legal rights and titles—interesting and sometimes important at law, but not really establishing anything more than property rights, as a rule. Character, ability, reliability, trustworthiness and other personal qualities are not in the least guaranteed in this way—now that the ancient principle of *noblesse oblige* is out of date. The principle works both ways: a good institution needs no minute historical justification; the presence and the power of the Living God in a church, in its leadership, in its ongoing, creative activity is more conclusive than chests full of fading documents.

It is the assumption of this book that the Roman primacy really got under way in the fifth century, not before; and that it was a providential turning point in history when this took place. The benefits to society, to the new nations of the North and West, and even in some degree to the older ones in the East, far outweighed the disasters that a few unworthy later popes brought upon the church, upon society in general, and upon themselves. The preceding four centuries, during which the papacy gradually took form and assumed the leadership signalized by Pope Leo the Great, are difficult to describe. The scattered and fragmentary references to the papacy do not add up to what might be expected or what many have claimed. If we take for our own Von Ranke's famous rule—he was the first great historian of the papacy, and the father of modern historical writing—and attempt to write as he did *die Geschichte wie es eigentlich gewesen* (history as it really took place), we

shall be at a loss to fill in many a lacuna during these dark
centuries. But that is the way it is, in ancient history. The
apologist will find it easy to leap from one stepping stone
to another and pretend a strong bridge is built above them;
but we know better. The present age demands hard, scien-
tifically demonstrable facts, not illusory fancies; and a romantic history of the past recalled from dreamland will not
suffice. Unless the history can be defended in the clear, cold
light of skeptical research, there is no use in advocating it.
Hence when we come to survey the rise of the papacy we
must take for granted nothing more than the ascertained
data prove.

But this is no more than is required of most research
into the past—and of all research where the data are scanty,
fragmentary, and scattered: the period of the "Judges" in
ancient Israel; the era of the tyrants in Greece, or the kings
in Rome; or the "blank page," as George Trevelyan calls
it, in Britain's early history. Take the last named for example; it closely parallels the rise of the papacy. We know
almost nothing of the Anglo-Saxons who destroyed the last
vestiges of Roman power in Britain. They were farmers,
and adventurers, from the shores of the Baltic and the
Saxon coasts of Jutland and Friesland. They had rude kings
and a rude nobility, and almost without arms they swarmed
upon and overwhelmed the weak defenders of towns and
villas in southern and eastern England. There are no authentic records of the Saxon conquest. The terrified Britons fled
westward into the mountains and glens of Wales, where
they reverted to their Celtic past. Lullingstone Villa in Kent
was plundered, and the large Christian medallions that
adorned it with their beautiful chi-rho designs (☧) fell
down inside its walls; the lavish mosaic floor of its dining
hall, with the four seasons at the four corners, was buried

under the ruins for fifteen centuries to come; and all this happened to dozens of other peaceful homes in the South, the East, and the North. The lament of Gildas, the sixth century Welsh bard and priest, is almost the sole record of the event: "Every colony is levelled to the ground. . . . The inhabitants are slaughtered. . . . Of the refugees who flee to the hills, some are captured and slain in heaps, others, starving, submit to lifelong slavery. . . . Still others, with bitter wailing, flee across the sea."

What can the historian make of the period? He has archaeology to help him, to some extent. But accurate record has he none. As Trevelyan writes,[2]

The historian has two points of light, and even those are dim. He sees an orderly Romano-Celtic world late in the fourth century, beginning to fall into chaos. Two hundred years later he sees a Saxon-Celtic barbarism beginning to emerge confusedly into the renewed twilight of history, and he hears the marching chaunt of St. Augustine and his monks bringing back with them the Latin alphabet and the custom of written record. Between these points stretches a great darkness. . . . The chief names of this missing period of history—Hengist, Vortigern, Cerdic, Arthur—may be those of real or of imaginary men. All that archaeology and history together can do is to indicate—not the date, leaders, landings, and campaigns—but only the general character of the warfare that destroyed Roman Britain and gave the land to the English.

The early history of the papacy is almost as difficult to reconstruct as that of early Britain during the Saxon period. Its leading figures are not, perhaps, as vague as King Arthur and the Table Round, but are more like the long series of royal figures adorning the west front of Lincoln Cathedral.

2. *A Shortened History of England*, London, 1959, p. 41.

Fabulous kings they were; but they must indeed have been *like* that, to have led the forward advance of civilization in their kingdoms!

Now of course the parallel is not exact. Britain was on the outskirts of the civilized world; Rome was its heart. But the problems of the historian are similar in the two cases. The theory of an orderly process of setting up a system of ecclesiastical supervision and rule is as impossible to prove as it is to trace the settlement of the Saxons in England and their slow conversion to Christianity, the history of their churches and their books, the Round Table of King Arthur, and the wise laws of King Alfred and his translation of the Bible. We know they were there—but where, and when, and how, and for how long, and of what nature and character? All these questions are beyond the range of the most diligent research. So with the papacy. More claims were made for it during the four hundred years preceding Pope Leo I; but also fewer—for some of the Bishops of Rome seemed quite uninterested in the subject of far-reaching ecclesiastical sovereignty. Yet the movement continued, like an army, marching not day and night, but for three days, then resting, then resuming, satisfied if the average comes up to ten miles a day (that is, it was so in the days before mechanized advance). But one must be on his guard not to read into the fragmentary records and reflections more than it is fair to read; and if one views the historian's task as a sacred office, a priestly ministry to divine truth, he must firmly reject the plaster and sawdust "filler" that has gone into much of the reconstruction of early papal history. This includes not just the fanciful golden dream of the Donation of Constantine, but whole pages and chapters of "history as it might have been," or, as some theologians may say, "as it *ought* to have been," in accordance with later dogma and theory. The picturesque, imaginative reconstruction of the usual story-book "history" is interesting, but it reflects the naïve faith of the writer and his contemporaries (or his parishioners) far more accurately than it does the actual, factual course of events *wie es eigentlich gewesen*. In the long run, "*truth* is great, and stronger than all things" (1 Esdr. 4.35 RSV) and it will, in the end, prevail over fiction and fantasy. We weaken and stultify divine truth when we patch up the record and make it completer than it ever was. The church needs no such support, any more than the sacred ark required the steadying hand of Uzzah (2 Sam. 6.6). God is still "keeping watch above His own," and our chief concern ought to be, not to rewrite the past, but to make the present correspond to the divine intention. If the papacy is a divine institution, and many of us will grant this without submitting to Rome, then the strongest evidence of this fact will be its positive, constructive "work for God" (*opus Dei*) in these days, not its flamboyant claims in the fifth or the eleventh or the thirteenth or the nineteenth century. The claims can rest, whether admitted or denied; the real evidence is pragmatic, and *now*. The truth of the claim is not to be proved by ancient texts, nor denied if they are lacking or inconclusive. The principle may be illustrated from the history of almost every religion in the world, past or present. A bold recognition of this principle, on all sides, would do more to clear the air for "ecumenical dialogue" than any amount of theological debate or maneuvering.

Let us admit then that the evidence for the papal primacy in the early Christian centuries is singularly weak and could scarcely pass muster among secular historians. In particular the New Testament texts upon which the primacy is supposedly based simply do not support it. And it is difficult to discover the relevance of many of the patristic passages cited, for example those listed in the Indices of Denzinger's *Enchiridion Symbolorum* [3] or de Journel's *Enchiridion Patristicum*.[4] The background of papal authority was chiefly the eminence and importance of the Roman see, the city of Rome, as capital of the world and for many centuries the seat of imperial authority. For example, it is often said that the first appeal to Petrine authority was the reply of Pope Stephen I (254-7) to St. Cyprian and the African bishops on the subject of the re-baptism of heretics. Stephen simply cited the ancient tradition and custom as authoritative. As Eusebius said, in his *History of the Church* (7.3.1), "Stephen, holding that they ought not to make any innovation contrary to the ancient tradition (*tēn kratēsasan archēthen paradosin*), was very indignant at the proposal."

Stephen's views were certainly sound, and his position indubitably correct. But where does his authority as pope, or his gift of infallibility, come in? It was Firmilian and others who described his decision as made *quasi Apostoli* ("as if he were an Apostle")—since Firmilian opposed the decision, the term is sarcastic, and he next referred to the pope as "Stephanus and those who agreed with him." The main question, for Firmilian and for Cyprian and for Eusebius and for the bishops of Cilicia, Cappadocia, Galatia, and other provinces, was whether or not reconciled heretics must be baptized (i.e. re-baptized following their heretical baptism, as Cyprian held), not the primacy or authority of the bishop of Rome. If we are to study sources and interpret them in a genuinely historical way, without special pleading or a defense of preconceived views, many of these proof texts will have to be abandoned. The standard of his-

3. 32d ed., 1963, pp. 843f, 847-50.
4. 22d ed., 1962, p. 777.

tory to be described *wie es eigentlich gewesen* will not tolerate such trimming, stretching, or forcing of evidence. Such language as that of Boniface I in 422, *Manet beatum Apostolum Petrum* ("The blessed Apostle Peter remains"),[5] claiming jurisdiction over the Orient, or that of the *Donation of Constantine*,[6] *beatissimo pontifici, patri nostro Silvestrio, universali papae* ("The most blessed Pontiff, our Father Sylvester, universal pope"), merely reflects the attitudes, ideas, and courtesy of the time. Nothing can be proved theologically or historically from such choice of words.

It is not even certain that Peter ever saw Rome, though many modern historical scholars incline to accept the view as probable, even without adequate evidence (see Ch. I). The earliest testimony is that of Clement of Rome in his letter to the Corinthians (1 Clement 5-6; ca. A.D. 96 or 98), where the apostolic examples of heroic martyrdom are cited:

Through jealousy and envy the greatest and most righteous pillars of the church were persecuted and contended even unto death. Let us set before our eyes the good apostles: Peter, who because of wicked jealousy suffered not merely one or two but many trials, and having thus borne his testimony went to his deserved place of glory. Through jealousy and strife Paul bore off the prize of endurance: seven times he was in bonds; he was exiled; he was stoned; he was a herald in both East and West and earned the noble fame of his faith; he taught righteousness throughout the world; and coming to the far limits of the West he bore testimony before the rulers, and so passed from this world and was taken up into the Holy Place—the very greatest example of endurance. To these men with their holy lives was

5. Denzinger, §§ 234f; Mirbt, § 155.
6. Mirbt, § 228, p. 112, line 13.

gathered a great multitude of the elect [the chosen] who were also victims of jealousy and showed among us the supreme example of endurance under outrage and torture.

Ignatius of Antioch, writing to the Christians at Rome as he likewise was being led to martyrdom there, ca A.D. 110, said (Ep. Rom. 4.3), "I do not command you, as did Peter and Paul; they were Apostles, I am a convict; they were free, I am still a slave." Such fragmentary and tantalizing evidence is not sufficient to prove Peter's residence in Rome and his martyrdom there, though it leaves open the probability that he died in Rome. As for a continued ministry in Rome covering twenty-five years, as the first pope, this is most improbable. Peter's departure for "another place" (*eis heteron topon* in Acts 12.17, echoed in 1 Clement 5.4) cannot mean his departure for Rome, in view of his presence in Jerusalem scarcely more than two chapters later (15.7), and also in view of the whole chronology of the New Testament, so far as we can make it out. The appeal to 1 and 2 Peter as authentic writings of the Apostle is growing steadily less confident among the literary experts. Moreover, the presupposition that Peter and Paul "founded" the church in Rome is refuted by Paul's Epistle to the Romans: (a) there were Christians in Rome before Paul got there, even before he wrote to them; and (b) Paul never mentions Peter as head of the Roman church. The whole theory is historically as valueless as the modern Roman guide's description of the little altar in the church of Santa Pudenziana as the one "where St. Peter said his daily mass." The legend of Peter's residence in Rome is consequently viewed by some modern historians as on a par with that of Joseph of Arimathea and the holy thorn of Glastonbury— a similar attempt to trace an apostolic origin.

Further, on the basis of First Clement, one cannot argue that monarchical episcopacy had reached Rome by 96 or 98, the date of that epistle to the church in Corinth. Accordingly, as Kurt Aland observes in his valuable article "Papsttum" in the new edition of *Die Religion in Geschichte und Gegenwart* (V, 51ff), the appointment of Peter's successors is out of the question: the list is as legendary as that of the most ancient kings of Britain or France. Nor is any bishop mentioned in Ignatius's letter to the church in Rome (in 110, i.e. a dozen years later): he writes to "the beloved and enlightened church—which has the pre-eminence in the country of the land of the Romans ... pre-eminent in love," and later he writes the same letter "to all the churches" (4.1). Even Irenaeus's list of bishops of Rome (see Ch. I), now viewed by some as partly fictitious, was drawn up under pressure of great need as the church faced the Gnostic crisis, in order to offset the Gnostic claim to a *secret* tradition handed down from the Apostles. Only the open and public succession of Catholic bishops could refute this: their witness agreed that the true tradition was the Catholic one, not the phantasmagorian speculations of the Gnostics. Of course there were bishops, as heads and leaders of the churches; but the lists are fragmentary, incomplete, and questionable, derived from well-remembered names of godly Christians and martyrs from the early days onward. Not until almost the middle of the third century can we be quite sure of the names—what went before was often imaginary. Such is the fate of legendary history, orally transmitted, everywhere in the ancient world, in Greece and Rome, in the Bible, and in the church.

Some of the facts reported about the early Roman church are highly creditable. Eusebius, in his *History of the Church* (6.43.11), reports that it counted "a great multitude" of baptized members in the days of Pope Cornelius (A.D. 251-3), all under one bishop, forty-six presbyters, seven deacons (as in Acts 6.5), seven subdeacons, forty-two acolytes, fifty-two exorcists; and it supported more than fifteen hundred widows and poor, "all of whom are cared for with the grace and charity of the Lord." Modern estimates of the total membership favor about thirty thousand. Evidently the church in Rome was true to its title of honor, conferred by St. Paul (Romans 1.8): "Your faith is proclaimed in all the world"—and it was still a "faith working through love" (Gal. 5.6). The first really monarchical bishop was Victor (189-99?), though the earliest evidence for the authority of the monarchical bishop over the presbyters and deacons is in Hippolytus's *Apostolic Tradition* 2-9 (ca. 215), though, as Aland remarks, it probably already existed in the second half of the second century. It is the remarkable growth of the church in Rome that is echoed in Eusebius's phrase "a great multitude": this was precisely the phrase used by Tacitus in describing the martyrs in Rome under Nero (*Annals* 15.44), *multitudo ingens*. It is the phrase also used by Clement, and by the Roman Gospel of Mark (3.7 and often).

The extraordinarily close relation of the church in Rome with other churches was doubtless inherent in its location and, after the time of Constantine, in its close association with the government. The close relation with Corinth could be partly due to trade and commerce, which have been media of Christian propagation and expansion more than once in the long course of the church's life. Moreover, Corinth was now a Roman colony and capital of the Province of Achaia. The idea of a special privilege divinely conferred upon Rome could have led to the creation of a "golden legend" to connect the brilliant present with the

glorious past—something likewise not unknown in human
history, both ecclesiastical and secular. In the second century, saints and heretics, mountebanks and philosophers
congregated in Rome, as today they still establish themselves there and in London, Paris, and New York. A foot-
hold in Rome meant a far greater leverage in propaganda
than a *pied-à-terre* anywhere else, even in any of the ancient cities of the Near East. The whole anti-Gnostic strategy of the church encouraged the centering of apostolic
tradition in the greatest see of all, in the capital of the
world; and it also encouraged the centering of apostolic
authority, the right to adjudicate differences, even in the
East, e.g. the Paschal controversy in the time of Victor
(189-99). As civil and political questions and cases were
brought to Rome for settlement, so were ecclesiastical.
Even though the early popes were not outstanding theologians, cases were submitted to them: as always and everywhere, the best mediators are not necessarily those most
learned in the law, but those who know what the law is
and have good sense in administering it. This skill or advantage based on experience reflects, not a constitutional
"primacy," but rather the natural course of development
in the growing world-church of Catholic Christianity—a
development that can be whole-heartedly regarded as divinely guided, without appeal to the New Testament or
the early fathers, or to their peculiar and fanciful exegesis.
But steadily the papal claims were becoming more articu-
late and mandatory, until eventually they culminated in the
position of the great Leo I.

Pope Leo's position in the West was creative and indispensable, if history was to go on and civilization escape
reversion into barbarism. When Constantine removed the
seat of empire to his "New Rome" on the Bosporus, the

West was left all but disarmed and helpless before the on-coming multitudes of wild invaders. The pragmatic dem-onstration of papal superiority or primacy, coupled with sound judgment and heroic determination, did more to es-tablish the papal "claims" than dozens of theological argu-ments. As we have seen, the pope really *was* the head of Christendom, in the West, and the first of bishops, the divinely appointed and endowed leader of the civilized world in its struggle for survival. The use and interpreta-tion of the Petrine texts found in the New Testament was only a rationalization: the genuine and ample proofs of the papal primacy were open to the eyes of all men. The claims of other, equally ancient, sees to a leadership at least on a par with Rome's were of no avail. Jerusalem counted for zero after the first century. Christianity was only a dwin-dling Jewish sect in its homeland. Caesarea rated little more. Antioch was in eclipse. Ephesus and the other "churches of Asia," like Alexandria in Egypt, were deeply entangled in theological quarrels—as we have already seen. Cappadocia was too remote and too late to influence even Byzantium, let alone the West. Constantinople was too new, too lack-ing in prestige, too dependent on the emperor's good will, to exercise much influence on Christendom. The whole drift and tendency of the age was westward (Constantine had grievously miscalculated!), and the whole future of Europe lay there and in the North. The very independence of the Carthaginian leaders, Cyprian, for example, and Augustine, contributed to the full development of the papal primacy: when such a church as theirs could be ex-pected to consult with Rome and take advice freely, the implication was obvious. Appeals to Rome were not infre-quent, but not always supported at home. Yet the general tendency was to defer to Rome's wisdom and authority—

itself a mark of wisdom, in view of the troubled times. Leo I dealt with Africa as if it were a part of Italy, not merely because that is the way the legates and lawyers had treated it under the early empire, but because the Vandals were sweeping the country, and the church was fighting for its life.

The schisms in the early Roman church were scarcely compatible with either an infallible church or a supreme ecclesiastical authority. But one can argue the same for the centuries that followed: the antipopes at Avignon, the split between East and West, the great schism between North and South effected by the Reformation. The *practical* objections to the theory of papal primacy and infallibility are decisive, for many persons. But for others the eventual success of the papal claims in the first five centuries, and later, and even now in prospect, if Vatican II succeeds, outweighs all objections from the pragmatic angle.

The concurrence of the two references, 1 Clement 5.1-7 and Ignatius, Rom. 4.3, to which the Ascension of Isaiah 4.2f should perhaps be added, seem to point toward Peter's death in Rome; but the date is not given. The reference to the Christian martyrs in Tacitus, *Annals* 15.44, names no names, and the tradition of Peter's burial on the Vatican Hill is not unanimously supported by ancient statements or by modern archaeology. The *Liber Pontificalis* maintains that the popes before Victor were buried "next to the body of Blessed Peter *in Vaticano*." But the archaeological finds do not support this statement. Presumably the early clergy of Rome were buried in the cemetery of S. Callistus.

Further, the saying in Matthew 16.18 presupposes a unique and untransferable office, and therefore cannot refer to a succession; the Gospel of Matthew is late, not early,

and reflects tradition, perhaps at Antioch, from a date presumably late in the first century, if not early in the second.[7]
Its tradition is Eastern, not Western, in all probability, and
is therefore all the more valuable for the presuppositions of
the Petrine saying. Many modern scholars view the saying
as post-Resurrection in date: Peter was the first to recognize the Risen Lord (1 Cor. 15.5) and the first to confess
his faith in Christ. But the founding of the church is still
in the future ("I will build"), i.e. it is eschatological, though
the subject of the church had no place among the eschatological sayings of Jesus found elsewhere in the gospels, and
the saying quoted here refers to eschatological conditions:
the "powers of death" and "the gates of hell" are clearly
eschatological conceptions. This church is a supernatural
institution, and is essential to Christian salvation. But it is
not even Peter the man who is the foundation of the church
(the Catholic interpretation), nor Peter's faith (the Protestant intepretation), but *the divine revelation* which has
inspired Peter's words: "Flesh and blood [human cogita-
tion] has not revealed this to you, but my Father who is
in heaven." Hence Christ pronounced Peter blessed, the
thought of a "foundation" being suggested by his name,
Petros, which means "rock." This is a common Semitic
turn of thought, as in 1 Chronicles 22.9f and other passages,
especially in the naming of the patriarchs and their children.
Peter is blessed *because* he has received the divine revelation of Christ's true nature and office. And his office as
holder of the keys does not denote his authority to admit
or expel or reject those who would enter the Kingdom of
Heaven. As the rest of verse 19 clearly shows, and also the
common usage of the figure in ancient Jewish idiom, it

7. See the evidence in my book, *The Gospels, Their Origin and Their
Growth*, New York and London, 1957.

means Peter's authority to make binding or to relax the rules governing the administration of the church and the conduct of believers, and also to pronounce "judgment" upon cases submitted to the church (as in ch. 18.18—and perhaps also in 18.19, according to the Syriac, which reads, "about anything *they shall be asked*.") It was a far cry from this original meaning of the passage to the use made of it, down the centuries, in the interest of the papal primacy. But the primacy needs no such support, and it is high time the false exegesis was discarded.

As Erich Dinkler says in his important article, "Petrustradition" in the new edition of *Die Religion in Geschichte und Gegenwart*, V, 261-63, three steps were involved in anchoring the Petrine primacy firmly to the text of the New Testament. These steps are reflected in Matthew 16. 17-19 ("Thou art Peter"), John 21.15 ("Feed my sheep"), and Luke 22.31f ("Strengthen thy brethren"). In each case there are important questions to be considered: (a) the authenticity of the tradition behind the saying, (b) its interpretation as referring to the apostolic see, and (c) its application to the succession of bishops in one particular see, that of Rome. Hence the importance of locating not only the see of Peter but also his tomb at Rome. After a clear, well-defined, precise statement of the evidence for the location of Peter's tomb under St. Peter's, Professor Dinkler asks for a Scot's verdict of "not proven." Wherever first interred, the relics of Peter and Paul were later transferred to other sites. Considering the difficulty of bodies buried in earth, especially in damp clay, the probability of finding the bones of St. Peter under the *Confessio* in St. Peter's seems less probable every century. Moreover, it is quite improbable that the martyred Christians were buried in Nero's Gardens, where they died, or among the

aristocratic tombs that lined the north side of the Via
Cornelia. According to Tacitus, they belonged to the "scum
of the earth." But the true situation is not any supposed
dependence of the papal primacy on the place of Peter's
burial, despite its rich and greatly treasured meaning for
Catholic devotion; instead, it rests upon the indubitable
leadership of the papacy through the centuries. The question of Peter's grave cannot possibly shake the foundations
of the most important spiritual office in the Western world.

Neither archaeology, then, nor the citation of ancient
texts, either from the early Church Fathers or from the
New Testament, add much in the way of support to the
legendary beginnings of the papal primacy. Yet it origi-
nated somewhere, sometime, historically, and it grew steadily until it emerged fully developed on the world scene.
Peter was undoubtedly a leader in the early Palestinian
Christian church, a missionary and a teacher, not the head
of the Jerusalem church (that was James the Lord's brother,
as in Acts 15), but certainly a leader of great influence.
Thus the book of Acts (chs. 1-12 and 15) clearly shows,
at one end of the tale, and the *Clementine Homilies* and
Recognitions (based on a *Grundschrift* or source from the
early third century—before 230) at the other end unite
in reporting. His missionary field was the Jewish area (see
Galatians 2.9 and Acts 9.32–12.17), not the Gentile field,
which belonged to Paul and others.[8] The very arrangement
of the Catholic Epistles in our New Testament witnesses
to the probable order of priority, rank, or position of the
presumed authors in the apostolic church: the order is
James, Peter, John, Jude. (The order of the books of the

8. Karl Heussi's view, based on Gal. 2.6, that Peter died early is not
generally held. See his book *Die römische Petrustradition in kritischer
Sicht*, Tübingen, 1955, pp. 1-10.

New Testament have something to tell us of the history of their composition, as I have argued in the case of the gospels: their original order in the manuscripts, which was also their order of composition, was, I believe, Mark, Luke, Matthew, John.[9])

It is not a question of new and improved translations of the New Testament; though the use of modern translations based on critical editions of the Greek text, on modern works in lexicography, grammar, and syntax, and on scholarly exegesis are a great advantage. The use of the *Revised Standard Version*, for example, which is now widely used by Protestants and others throughout the English-speaking world, and is presently to appear in Great Britain in a Catholic edition, is a mark of advancing scholarship in biblical studies. But the main thing is to *study* the scriptures, to "search" them (Jn. 5:39), if we would arrive at a full understanding of the relation of the scriptures to the church, its traditions and its teaching. This is equally as important as is private study for purposes of edification, as in the pietist Bengel's famous saying: *Te totum applica ad textum: rem totum applice ad te:* "Apply yourself wholly to the text; then apply the text wholly to yourself." This great saying appears at the beginning of every copy of Nestle's edition of the Greek New Testament. Nevertheless, "no prophecy of scripture is a matter of one's own interpretation" (2 Pet. 1.20). Christianity, like Judaism upon which it is based, is a *social* religion, not a cult of private devotion, meditation, and pursuit of spirituality. When the great creeds came to be formulated, they began, "*We believe* in one God. . . ." [10] So it is with the crucial passages before us

9. See my book, "*The Gospels, Their Origin and Their Growth*, New York and London, 1957, especially ch. VI.
10. Bettenson, pp. 34-7; Denzinger, §§ 40-51, 71.

in the New Testament. "Strengthen thy brethren" surely
implies the solidarity and security of the group of disciples;
it also implies Peter's leadership and responsibility at the
beginning of the Christian movement. The full story is not
told, but it is clearly implied that there *was* a story. "Feed
my sheep" goes even further and attributes to Peter a permanent office, not merely a momentary strategic act of
rallying his fellow disciples. But it says nothing of a succession of Peter's relations or descendants, which would
have been a normal and perfectly natural arrangement in
a Semitic environment, and was apparently presupposed by
some in the early church: note James's headship of the Jerusalem church in Acts 15 and the story of Jude's grandsons
related by Eusebius in his *History of the Church* 3.19f and
32; some historians have even referred to the "Jerusalem
caliphate!" Nor does the passage refer to any succession of
chosen officials as successors to St. Peter. The whole outlook is still eschatological, even in the Fourth Gospel.
There is almost no future to count upon: *these* are the
"latter days" foretold by the prophets—this theme runs
through the whole New Testament. But it is the situation
out of which the permanent headship grew, with bishops,
then metropolitans, and, finally, in the West, a supreme
pontiff, the pope. Off in the distance we see dimly outlined
figures moving through the early morning mist, like shep-
herds on the far hills. They are real. They are alive and
moving. They are going somewhere. Would that the story
were more detailed!

IX

Unfinished Business of
the Vatican Council

There are no absolute beginnings in history. Always there are antecedents and favorable conditions and mounting crises and new ideas or tendencies that began a generation or two before the event, which finally emerges new and apparently unique and transforming. History is like a broad, mysterious, unexplored river that sweeps down from the dense forests of the past. As we look back on the nineteenth century we can see what led to the First Vatican Council; but the forces and conditions must be traced further back than 1800, at least back to 1789, or even earlier. For the First Vatican Council was an attempt to consolidate a crumbling front, to erect a barrier against cataclysmic change and revolution. The French Revolution, like an earthquake, had spawned tremors and geological adjustments and further revolutions all over Europe, eventually all over the world. It released Napoleon and his wars, like the threatening horror from the pit in the Book of Revelation. The Congress of Vienna (1815) was expected to settle all disputed questions, but it settled none, at least none permanently. The repeated revolutions in Paris and the upheaval in Germany in the 1840's and the colossal changes in central Europe that led to the *Anschluss* of 1866 and the Dual Monarchy and the Franco-Prussian War—all these facts and factors belong to the background of Vatican I. The *Syllabus of Errors* and the dogma of papal infallibility were really inspired by an effort to stem the colossal tide of the times, a tide of change in politics, economics, social order, religion, and philosophy. The pope, Pius IX, who began as a liberal, was suddenly cured of his liberalism when the church lost the Papal States. Henceforth, he favored reaction, especially after his two years of exile at Gaeta. But change was sweeping the earth, irresistibily, and even these drastic measures could not counter it. In 1869 most of the French army was withdrawn from Italy and returned home to prepare for the defense of France against Prussia. Instead of Garibaldi and his Piémontese, the new Italian army under General Cadorna moved into Rome, and the Council came to a swift and sudden end on October 20, 1870. Its adjournment was *sine die*. Its agenda was far from completed; only two of the proposed schemata had been considered, and the definition of papal infallibility was not balanced by a definition of the powers and responsibilities of the bishops, which were to have been considered next. Frustrated, truncated, adjourned almost as soon as it had got under way (in the leisurely manner of old-fashioned councils), the Vatican Council never reassembled. Instead of the view that has prevailed in some quarters, the truth is that Vatican II was not designed to continue and complete the unfinished work of Vatican I. It was designed to be an independent council, with new agenda all its own. Thus instead of being a continuation of Vatican I, the problems, tendencies, conditions and events lying behind and leading up to Vatican II fill the whole century since the earlier Vatican Council:

it is a body of fresh problems, new and different, and yet related to those which had led to Vatican I. There really are no breaks in historical continuity. The unfinished business of Vatican I is after all still on the table, and to it has now been added a longer list of agenda.

The great vision of Pope John XXIII was not limited to Christian reunion, though it certainly embraced it. First and foremost there was to be a refreshing, revitalizing "updating" of the Roman Catholic Church itself, before reunion could be either proposed or considered. And the intended *aggiornamento* of the Roman Catholic Church must surely have been expected to inspire a like effort on the part of the rest of Christendom, Protestant, Orthodox, and Anglican. For a generation now, we have heard the ringing cry of the ecumenical leaders, Archbishop William Temple and others, especially some of the Continental theologians: "Let the Church be the Church!" Only a church that is willing to be, under God, the *church*, not a political organization or arm of the state, or a civic betterment association, or a perpetual revivalist campaign, or a propaganda institute for reactionary theological and social views (they go together)—only the purely religious society of the followers of Jesus, devoted to living and teaching the Christian way of life, the Christian faith, the moral standards and outlook of the gospel, the "philosophy" of Christ (as some of the Victorians called it)—only such a church can face the problems of today with any hope of solving them. Pope John's idea, like Archbishop Temple's, was really revolutionary! And some of the conservatives in Rome and elsewhere fully realized it from the day he first explained his plan.

This brief preliminary sketch of the background is indispensable for an understanding of Vatican II—this, or

some other and better sketch, not to mention the fully detailed knowledge of the period by a careful historian, who
will understand best of all. Many persons have asked, what
has the Council accomplished? Others, what terms does
Rome lay down for reunion? Others, has Rome changed,
or is she preparing to change, her theology or organization
or program for religious world-dominion? These questions
either cannot be answered or, if partial answers are attempted, they can be considered only from the point of
view of the ongoing situation, the changing scene of world
events, after two world wars and now a third, a "cold" war
that grows hotter from time to time. What if the church
should turn out to have the real and only solution of our
problems? Once upon a time it had a solution, in the fifth
century. When the papacy really got under way it swung
its batteries—or its radar—ninety degrees to the left, from
Constantinople and the East to the new nations in the
North, the vast barbarian populations then settling down
in Gaul and Germany and the Low Countries—settling
down, but at the same time menaced by attack from other
barbarians in their rear, whose needs were also attended to
in a short time by the missionary efforts of the church.
Under Leo the Great the Roman papacy was a godsend to
all mankind, especially in the West and North. It achieved
a purpose which was so obvious no one could have in-
vented it, but which no one hitherto had possessed the
courage to undertake. All the later history of Europe was
to share in the blessings of this period and its outstanding
leader. In spite of later mistakes and frequent indolence,
blunders, and indifference, wrong choices and worse motives on the part of a few men unworthy of their great calling and opportunity, the papacy continued to be the most
powerful institution for good, for peace and social har-

mony, for education and welfare, in all the long centuries since civilization first arose in the West.

But can the church repeat the miracle? One wonders, and hopes, and prays that it may do so. For the steady barbarization of our world today is fully as bad as it was in the third, fourth, and fifth centuries—say from the economic panic and decline under Decius, beginning about the year 250. The pages of Gibbon, and of Gregory of Tours, can easily be matched and illustrated with a multitude of clippings from the daily newspaper, every day in the year! The literature of today is replete with laments matching those of Venantius Fortunatus and Rutilius Namatianus. Even the great Augustine, watching the Vandals ravage and destroy his diocese in North Africa, can be matched by religious leaders today—in Southeast Asia, in South Africa, in the Congo, and even in places nearer to us. (No place on earth is remote, any longer.) The collapse of honesty and integrity at high levels of responsibility and at low ones, the open defense of greed and selfishness as something forced upon us, as natural in human behavior as eating and sleeping—this is the deepest and most corrupt root of our world-wide disease today. I was talking with a friend in Rome one day: "How do you like our new pope?" he asked. I replied that I thought Pope John was God's special gift to our generation. "But," he continued, "don't you think he is pretty far to the left?" Yes, I said, perhaps he is; but no further to the left than St. Paul, and certainly our Lord—the discussion was abruptly ended, never to be resumed. Man must face it: his own greed, avarice, selfishness, irresponsibility, his unconcern for all but the most immediate demands upon him—this is what has created our crises hitherto, and still continues to create them. I do not know any other organization than the Christian church,

any other movement, any other idea, any other principle
that promises the slightest help out of this bottomless morass
in which we are now floundering, but only the Christian
religion, if stripped to its bare essentials and turned loose
upon society. The oldest institution in our world is still the
Christian church. But it is not doing its best work, it is not
exercising its proper influence and example, it is not even
pulling its own weight. What it could, and should, be
doing is a sharp contrast to what it is actually accomplish-
ing. Cannot the church be roused, and made effective once
more, and inspired to undertake the task of teaching and
healing the nations? That is what Pope John asked the
cardinals to consider when, in January 1959, he first proposed an ecumenical council. It was an inspired proposal,
even to John himself, and certainly to millions of Christians
everywhere.

   One of the most encouraging features of the present
council is the number of speeches on the subject of the
nature of the church as a mystical entity, purely supernatural in essence, and nothing less than the spiritual Body
of Christ. This is a "pastoral" approach, which Pope John
enjoined, and it has more promise for wide understanding
and vital reinforcement of the church's mission than all the
rubrics and canons in the official books—necessary as many
of them are. The Council has steered away from a rigidly
juridical point of view, just as Pope John bade it do, and
has frequently adopted this more mystical, supernatural,
theocentric conception. The Church is more than an institution, more even than a channel of divine grace; it *is* the
life in grace, a supernatural life found here in this world,
even at the present time: an eternal life in the midst of time,
lived under the eye and by the power of God, as Adolf
Harnack defined it long ago. Perhaps all our problems need

to be reoriented before they can be solved: not on an anti-historical basis; nor even on an a-historical or non-historical basis, or an existential, as some propose; but on the basis of living, present experience. This has always been the foundation of true religion, not an echo from the past, not a code or a constitution adopted or authorized long ago, but the living, first-hand experience of men and women who live in direct contact with God and share the life in grace day by day. For them the spiritual or supernatural is as real as tables and chairs, or oaks (as Plato said), or the summer sunshine. The truly spiritual *is* the supernatural, as Baron von Hügel insisted, and the moral, as Charles Kingsley said. It is no use arguing that, although this realm of spiritual, i.e. supernatural, reality is inaccessible at present, it was nevertheless open and accessible once upon a time, long ago; and that it must therefore be treated as infallibly authoritative, on the basis of its ancient record. For it means nothing to us, if we are shut out and denied access to it and imprisoned within a purely natural, mechanical, material world. This would be Gnosticism, with a vengeance!—a kind of Gnosticism that is wholly pessimistic, negative, fatalistic.

It is on the basis of the present spiritual experience of men and women that we ask to have the great dogmas set forth and explained, perhaps even defined, and authorized. For example, the doctrines included in Mariology; or the doctrine of the Real Presence of Christ in the Eucharist—of which Transubstantiation was once the magnificent illustration and explanation, on the basis of the Scholastic-Aristotelian physics, a marvelous poetic conception as much as a scientific one. So also might the doctrine of the Blessed Trinity be explained by appeal to experience, and given meaning once more, far closer to human needs than the remote mathematical formulae of theological speculation. The words *person* and *substance* are in reality only projections of human terms into an area beyond our capacity for conceiving, with the purpose of illustrating what cannot be fully described, let alone defined. And so with almost every other doctrine that presents problems today. As the pious author of the old *Theologia Germanica* affirmed,

> Blessedness lieth not in much and many, but in One and oneness. In a word, blessedness lieth not in any creature, or work of the creatures, but it lieth alone in God and in His works. Therefore I must wait only on God and His work, and leave on one side all creatures with their works, and first of all myself. In like manner all the great works and wonders that God has ever wrought or shall ever work in or through the creatures, or even God himself with all His goodness, so far as these things exist or are done outside of me, can never make me blessed, but only in so far as they exist and are done and loved, known, tasted and felt within me.[1]

In other words, what does it matter if God exists, unless I can know Him? What does it matter if Christ died for man's sins, if I cannot realize it?—unless I can be set free from the power of sin, and given the power not to sin henceforth? What does it matter if the Christian's life is hid with Christ in God, if I am unable to experience it? This or something very like this was the telling test of the mediaeval "Friends of God," those fourteenth-century Catholic pietists who so deeply influenced the really constructive leaders of the Reformation. It reflects a kind of "spiritual realism" which has always dominated Catholic theology, a present reality rather than a traditional or literary record of something experienced by others long

1. Translated by Susanna Winkworth; Andover, Mass., 1855, ch. IX, *ad fin.*

ago but now only a group memory or a faint whisper of some distant recollection, like what you remember of your grandfather's tales of his boyhood. It is this approach, and this presupposition of the ancient religious realism of the church, that promises a far more secure and reliable solution of theological problems than all the arguments men have advanced in the past fifteen centuries. And the same presupposition holds good for the moral convictions upon which a Christian society must be based—or any humane society, determined to achieve brotherhood and fellowship and justice rather than follow the *laissez faire* habit of letting greed and selfishness have full sway.

But, it will be pointed out, the church has never really launched out upon the deep and ventured to found its dogmas exclusively upon direct experience. It has always appealed to history, to scripture and to tradition, as well as to confirmatory experience, not to experience alone; and the appeal to experience has come last, not first, in order of presentation. The "spirituals," from St. Paul's generation at Corinth and the Montanists of the second century, to the later mediaeval and other groups claiming direct inspiration, as do some even today—these people and their claims have usually been rejected by the church. It is a pity if the extravagance and exaggeration of some have called in question a principle of the utmost importance, the one that has been in the background all along. The appeal to experience must be an appeal to the experience of the *whole* church, not to that of the private individual and a few of his ardent followers. It is not necessary to discard history—whether or not Cardinal Manning ever really said that "the appeal to history is treason!" The venture doubtless has its risks: there are many who will say, "*My* spiritual experience rules out, for example, the doctrine of the perpetual virginity

of the Blessed Virgin Mary, and also that of her bodily
assumption to heaven." Others may say, "The doctrine of
the Trinity is no part of *my* spiritual experience, and how
can it be that of anyone else? It is merely a scholastic,
intellectual, metaphysical construction worked out by philosophical dreamers in bygone ages." But the proposal to
base dogma upon present reality rather than upon ancient
records—or to test it by present reality *first*, before turning
to the ancient records, which are often obscure and also
fragmentary—must have a broader base, as we have suggested, than the experience of a few hundred individuals:
it must take as its foundation the continuous and universal
experience of the whole church, as in the appeal to the past
which St. Vincent of Lerins formulated: *Quod semper,
quod ubique, quod ab omnibus* [2]—"What [has been held]
always, everywhere, and by all."

For example, if the adoration of the Virgin, if prayers to
her, if confidence in her intercession, if the experience of
her mediation of divine grace is as ancient as the church,
and is found in every century and in every place, then the
dogma justifies itself, it rests upon a foundation of self-
evidencing truth and reality, and is no longer a matter of
theological debate or of biblical and patristic exegesis. The
extraordinary thing is that for Catholics the dogma does
reflect religious practice and experience, and in truth in-
spires it, by a reciprocal flow of devotion *cum* response
which is characteristic of all vital religion the world over
and from the most ancient times. It is, in fact, in this same
way that men have come to believe in the divinity, the
deity, the spiritual sovereignty of Christ—not by some
superstitious process of deification in the late Hellenistic

2. Bettenson, pp. 118-20; de Journel, § 2168.

age, basing it on miracles and legends. For Catholics, the dogma of the Mediation of the Blessed Virgin is a living faith; but for Protestants even the Virgin Birth is a dormant dogma, no real use being made of it either in the liturgy or in private devotion. But around the name of Mary, in Catholic devotion, has clustered a whole paradise of poetry, aspiration, confidence, faith, self-abnegation. Even among Anglicans there are those who, like the poet John Keble, address her with affectionate awe:

> *Ave Maria*, thou whose name
> All but adoring love may claim!

And in the modern hymnals, Anglican and other, Athelstan Riley's glorious hymn, *Ye Watchers and Ye Holy Ones*, is found and is sung with enthusiasm by multitudes—some of them perhaps without reading carefully the lines of the second verse:

> O higher than the cherubim,
> More glorious than the seraphim,
>   Lead their praises, Alleluia!
> Thou bearer of the eternal Word,
> Most gracious, magnify the Lord,
>   Alleluia, Alleluia, Alleluia, Alleluia
>   Alleluia!

Her "image" or "memory" has strengthened the weak, supported the desolate and forlorn, comforted the mourners, and solaced the starving, the tortured, and the martyred. The development of Mariology is largely unhistorical, in the sense that no appeal can be made to primary documents, though sometimes these are forced to bear a witness they would not normally provide: note the language of the New

Testament, such as "first-born son," "thy father and I," "the son of Joseph," and so on.

But the real support of the *Marienkultus* is the living devotion out of which the dogma arises, its answer to human need, the spiritual satisfaction it provides, its consonance with other Christian doctrines, its firmly dovetailed union with Christian ethics, especially the ethics of sex, motherhood, and family life. Even the dogma of the Assumption only rounds out the church's doctrine of the Incarnation. And, some would add, the Incarnation itself, as dogma, is derived from something far more urgent and personal than historical evidence. It rests upon the present reality of Christ's mediation, his revelation of the Father, his life-giving grace and power experienced within the church. You cannot really *prove* the Virgin Birth of Christ, or the Immaculate Conception of his Virgin Mother, or her Perpetual Virginity, or her Assumption, or the Mediatorial Office of *either* Christ or his Blessed Mother, certainly not by an appeal to ancient texts. The only real evidence is direct spiritual contact, within the Mystical Body, the living church, where this experience is cherished and promoted. As St. Paul expressed it, his own greatest aspiration in life was "to know [Christ] and the power of his resurrection" (Phil. 3.10). It was not to *see* Christ in heaven or at the Parousia (the "Second Coming"), but to *know* him, here and now. The same is true of those mystics and spiritual devotees who long to know his Blessed Mother, here and now, to communicate with her, to benefit by her intercessions, to be safeguarded by her presence and her prayers. From the point of view of the history of religions, there is no difference in principle between Mariolatry and Christolatry, the worship of the Blessed Virgin and the worship of her Son. As Christology rested largely upon the foundation of religious experience, enriching and confirming the faith derived from (or authenticated by) the New Testament documents, so Mariology has likewise developed. This fact must be frankly faced in "ecumenical" circles, however little many of us are inclined to accept it. The chief difference is that a Christological collection of writings was produced and preserved in the New Testament: there was no corresponding (or substitute) collection of Mariological documents. Those which appeared were far later in date, far less historical in content, and fewer in number. But the underlying development in religious thought and devotion was parallel, and continued for many centuries, and survives to this day, a powerful and widespread devotion in both East and West. We are not likely to get very far in the discussion of reunion with either Rome or the East if we refuse even to talk about Mariology.

It is of course a far cry from *Ave Maria, gratia plena* (cf. Luke 1.28) to the teaching that St. Mary is the sole mediatrix of divine grace. As we wish to argue, the doctrine has surely been arrived at on the basis of religious experience, not by way of exegesis of the New Testament or its translation. The very phrase *gratia plena* ("full of grace") is a poor translation of the Greek *kecharitōmenē*, a perfect passive participle, used as a vocative in lieu of the name of the person addressed, "O favored one" (Revised Standard Version) or "Most favored one" (New English Bible). As Fr. Max Zerwick beautifully says, in his *Analysis Philologica Novi Testamenti Graeci* (Rome, 1953), the word is "almost a proper name." St. Jerome was not to be trusted to bring out the true nuance of the word; his low views of womanhood, reflecting his wild experiences in youth, prevented his understanding and appreciation of this marvelous line in St. Luke's prose-poem. The phrase "full of grace" doubtless had some influence in encouraging the doctrine of the Virgin's mediation of grace; the doctrine could hardly have sprung from Luke 1.28 in Greek or in any adequate translation of the Greek. The fact remains, and remains significant, that there is no New Testament basis for the doctrine. What we have is "the New Testament of our Lord and Saviour Jesus Christ," not "a New Testament of our Lady." The surviving historical data for the beginnings of Mariology or Mariolatry are not adequate for the purpose to which they are put—for example, the popular picture of Pentecost, with the Virgin seated in the midst of the Apostles and receiving the central and most impressive portion of the divine gift of the Spirit. As poetry, as devotion, why not encourage it? As history, as fact, as doctrine, it suggests baseless fancy and speculation, to those who do not share the devotion. The doctrine of the mediation of all divine grace by the Blessed Virgin will be a most difficult, perhaps impossible, one for Protestants and Anglicans to accept, despite its advocacy by Rome and its wide spread in the East. When all is said and done, the dogma also, unfortunately, has weighted the scale on one side, that of the Docetic-Gnostic emphasis on celibacy and continence, and the substitution of the ideal of virginity for the Judaic and biblical (including New Testament) recognition of marriage and family life, the conception, birth, care and nurture of children as the ideal and norm of human sex relations.

As it appears to many Christians, the two dogmas, the Incarnation and the Virgin Birth (really two series of dogmas), sustain and throw light upon each other, as to both their origin and their present meaning and value. The appeal to ancient texts, and the stubborn limitation of dogmatic development to the New Testament, chronologically

arranged, or to the earlier oral or written sources underlying the New Testament, or even to the Church Fathers
down to Nicaea—any such limitation is pure *Historismus*,
unworthy of a living, ongoing, creative religious faith.
(The same charge would be made against any other religion.) It is no use, for example, to cite the Mother Goddess
of the ancient Mediterranean world, worshiped all the way
from Syria and Anatolia to Brittany and the British Isles,
and to maintain that Mary simply succeeded to this devotion as the church took over its heritage from prehistoric
paganism. I have often reflected upon the explanation
offered by a guide at Chartres who was showing us the
pagan statuette of the Mediterranean mother and child
found under the crypt of the cathedral: "You see, people
worshiped the Blessed Virgin long before Christ was born."
There is far more truth in that observation than one realizes
at first. It is not a generalization on the curious continuity
of the history of religions. It is an insight into the way
mankind apprehends spiritual reality. Only timidity refuses
to recognize that the worship of the Virgin is a part of the
total process of response to divine revelation; or to admit
that the recognition of her place in the totality of religious
life and thought is comparable with and a part of the general result of acknowledging the revelation of God in
Christ. It is not superstition, as some have held, though the
cultus may degenerate into superstition, as any cultus may;
instead, it is an essential and inalienable part of historic
Christianity, in both East and West.

The checks and tests of this principle of creative dogma,
or of the "creative evolution" of dogma, must include consistency with the original sources, i.e. the earliest records,
though they were not chiefly meant to be records. But this
consistency must not be understood as a bare, crude, logical

agreement; it must reach down to the very roots of the conceptions: What do we mean, or understand, by God, and by His self-revelation? Along with this must go the test of the fresh fruits of such a faith as it is manifested in the lives of believers. I doubt that St. Paul would have shared the view I am advocating, but he did not live twenty centuries later than the beginnings of the Christian religion. Yet I cannot imagine that he would have protested against it. The Master of us all had said, "By their fruits you shall know them." And the Apostle had written, "The fruits of the Spirit are love, joy, peace"—and all the Christian virtues.

The same principle applies to other doctrines. Some modern Protestant scholars have attempted to rest the doctrine of the Incarnation securely upon the so-called "messianic consciousness" of Jesus, supposedly reflected in the gospels and their underlying sources. But the total futility of such a plan should have been clear to all by 1901, when Wilhelm Wrede's *Messiasgeheimnis in den Evangelien* ("The Messianic Secret in the Gospels") appeared and also Albert Schweitzer's *Messianitäts- und Leidensgeheimnis* ("The Secret Messiahship and Passion"), and certainly by 1906 when his *Von Reimarus zu Wrede* ("From Reimarus to Wrede") was published, or by 1910, when the English translation, *The Quest of the Historical Jesus,* appeared in London. The experiment is still undertaken, from time to time, but it is hopeless. The only real ground for belief in the Incarnation is the ongoing life of the Church, its sacramental worship, the presence and power of the divine Lord Christ through the Holy Spirit resident in the community of Jesus' followers, the life in grace and the consequent transformation of human character, human aims, hopes, aspirations, affections, and strength of will that springs from the total "event" of Christ—as John Knox, Paul Tillich, and others use the term. The Incarnation is not an event in the remote past, nearly two thousand years ago; it is still a present fact, positive and apprehensible in the world right now. If this were not so, it would have ceased to be believed ages ago.

There are other doctrines that concern all Christians, not just Roman Catholics or any other group less than the totality of Christians in the world—in East and West, North and South, Old World and New, and the isles of the seven seas. These doctrines are not to be approached by any of us in a purely historical or a purely philosophical (speculative) or a purely exegetical or a purely moral or probabilistic way—as if Christian doctrine were a set of sanctions for moral behavior, whatever their ultimate truth. We must in fact go back some distance and start reconsidering our faith as if there still were a united Church, as if, let us say, Erasmus were our leader in a reform movement within Western Christendom, and the long centuries of turmoil since then were unheard of; as if the reform of the church "in head and members" were a real possibility without a schism or an explosion or a long battle around the walls of "Fortress Ecclesia" ending only in a vast proliferation of "Christian" sects, all in disagreement and led by disputatious theologians. If we can recapture this outlook of the fifteenth century (not the sixteenth), we may be able to go on from there.[3] But it will be a long time before real church unity is achieved. It may be a generation—it may be ten! Before we can achieve anything like genuine reunion we must have a long period of gradual reconciliation, fellowship, mutual understanding, and brotherhood. We

3. In the same way we should go back beyond 1054 in considering the problems of our brethren in the East.

must learn to work together, especially for causes that concern us all, and all mankind; we must learn to worship
together; we must read each other's books (most Roman
Catholics never read a Protestant religious book); we must
above all learn to trust each other and give each other
credit for the highest motives, not the lowest, and we must
cease spreading suspicion about the "separated brethren,"
whether Roman, Eastern, Protestant, or Liberal. It is almost
ludicrous, the facile hopes for reunion that we hear expressed today. Imagine a long-feuding neighborhood where
it is suddenly decided to stop the nonsense and at once to
arrange marriages between the most belligerent families.
Alas for the unhappy couples!

Again, the authoritative tone and attitude of the Roman
Catholic Church in stating Christian doctrines and moral
teachings, and requiring their acceptance as formulated by
Rome, will be difficult for all non-Roman-Catholic Christians to accept. Protestants are accustomed to an appeal to
holy scripture and to reason: "Let reason and the will of
God prevail" is a principle embedded in our tradition. It is
noticeable that in mission preaching and in apologetic writings the Roman Catholic Church often adopts a milder
tone, less dogmatic and more persuasive; but in decreeing
the faith and the moral teaching of the church to its faithful,
its loyal adherents, the tone is legalistic and imperative. For
example, the words used by the English hierarchy in repu-
diating the suggestion that the church recognize birth control and permit the use of contraceptive pills: "The Church
knows well that her children are undergoing a period of
great strain." [4] The outburst of protests against this would-be
sympathetic "father knows best" attitude is significant—and
is echoed far outside Great Britain. It is all too obvious that

4. *New York Times*, May 8, 1964.

Holy Mother Church is identified with the hierarchy, and that the church's unhappy "children" are the silent and passive laity, the "faithful." How long will conservatives continue to talk this way? Do they not realize that all baptized Christians are members of Christ, and that the moral responsibility of the ordinary Christian for his own personal, domestic, and social life is something inalienable and inseparable from his calling in Christ? Much as one loves and admires the Roman Catholic Church, there is nothing for us here but discouragement and frustration.

The whole question of birth control or, better, of family planning, is unavoidable in a world steadily becoming overpopulated. Some method of limiting population to numbers that can be fed, housed, clothed, and educated is not only a natural solution but a highly moral one. To fail to see this is a sign of moral blindness. The only possible method or the only one the church can authorize *may* be that of renunciation and self-restraint. As an eminent woman member of the Italian Chamber of Deputies said not long ago, "No one ever died of continence." But the tension and turmoil of family life where either there are far too many children, too close together, or the parents are trying to repress their own sex life to a level where the spacing of children is consonant with the family income, proves that something more effective than spiritual counsel is required. As Pope Pius XII was credited with saying, "God does not expect every family to have fifteen children." The words, "Be fruitful and multiply" (Genesis 1.28) were addressed to Adam and Eve in an empty world, not to the overcrowded nations of the present century. Protestants certainly demand a much fuller recognition of the rights and responsibilities of the laity than has been customary in

Roman Catholicism. After all, it is the lives of the laity that are being shaped and decided.

Speaking of the church's attitude toward the laity, one might say further that Rome seems to be too much concerned not to upset or "scandalize" the faithful, who must be very uneducated and unintelligent if they do not already know the problems that face them. Obviously, they are more aware of their problems than some of the hierarchy or even of the other clergy realize. Humanism is far more widely spread and much further advanced today than many of the theologically-minded among us, Catholic or Protestant, seem to recognize. The danger is not of a religious revolution, but of a silent abandonment of the old positions, like the melting away of a defeated army. Some of our own hierarchy and other leaders in the Protestant world live a life kept separate and apart from the rank and file of human beings, sometimes even apart from the majority of their own clergy. It is not celibacy alone that segregates religious leaders: clericalism, professionalism, an inability to comprehend what is the matter with people in trouble—this is by no means peculiarly Roman.

This separation from life is also sometimes manifest in a separation from scholarship and the problems of research. The attitude of the authorities toward the Pontifical Biblical Institute in Rome and even the École Biblique at Jerusalem is very disturbing to Protestants and Anglicans, who are used to free biblical research. It is not only that we believe in the "open Bible," from which we derive our doctrine; it is in our tradition, in our blood. Even before the Reformation there were biblical scholars asserting or assuming freedom of research: not only Wyclif, but Robert Grosseteste, the thirteenth-century Franciscan biblical scholar and bishop of Lincoln, who defended the rights of the clergy against king and pope alike; and Marsilius of Padua, his contemporary, the author of *Defensor Pacis*, who was the first to question the Petrine tradition, holding that Peter had no pre-eminence over the other Apostles, and that it is even doubtful if he was ever bishop of Rome, or even saw Rome, let alone was martyred and buried there. The attempt to prescribe in advance the results scholars must arrive at certainly indicates a standpoint that prefers the traditional formulation of theology to the fresh investigation of holy scripture.

Along with this goes the attempt to coerce editors and publishers, by threat of boycott—as I discovered when the *Encyclopaedia Britannica* delayed and finally, after three years, rejected a few articles the editor had asked me to prepare: they were unacceptable to the Roman Catholic censor of educational books, since they represented a "Protestant" view of the Bible. Along with this attitude goes also the discipline of teachers who read suspected books. In Rome, in 1963, I tried to call upon and pay my respects to an eminent New Testament scholar at the Gregorian University. I was unable to do so, as he was being "inhibited": he could eat in the refectory, I gathered, read in the library, write in his room, but not receive guests, talk with students, or teach classes. The inhibition resulted from his reading of works by Rudolf Bultmann—one of whose early books I had translated and urged students to read, over many years! Such tyranny may be explained from the dogmatic and legalistic point of view, but not from that of free scholarship. It would be unthinkable in a Protestant or Anglican seminary or university! It smacks of the Inquisition. It reflects a hierarchy overloaded on the Italian side. It also reflects a wholly antiquated view of biblical research and a fanciful view of history. And in the field of science the record is no better. It will be a long time before the silencing of Teilhard de Chardin is forgotten. What is it that possesses theologians and ecclesiastics with the desire to silence historians, scientists, exegetes, and one another?

One is scarcely encouraged by the more recent statement of the present pope, who severely warns biblical scholars against "a pernicious itch for newness" and the "rash opinions of innovators." Even the famous Cardinal Tisserant has dismissed as insignificant the divergence in wording of the four Gospels, which represents merely adaptation to "the varied conditions of the faithful." [5] One must speak plainly: such an attitude is diametrically opposed to that of many Protestants, and is totally incompatible with any hope for reunion, at least among the educated. It may even presage a decline in enthusiasm for the standards of the Roman Catholic Church within its own constituency, wherever liberal education and academic freedom are known.

The instinct to dominate and coerce is deeply rooted in human nature, and all churches tend to manifest it in one way or another. So is the instinct to judge others by oneself, one's own views and convictions. The test of Catholicity that Rome applies is naturally her own conception of its meaning, which on the whole is institutional and legal. Even as well-intentioned a book as Fr. George Tavard's *The Quest for Catholicity* (St. Louis, 1964) assumes that Anglicanism lacks—has lost—this quality and since the sixteenth century has been endeavoring to recover it, like some pitiful *famille nouveau-riche* in quest of social status and recognition. But a similar tale might be told of Rome's quest for Catholicity, ever since the fifth century, which

5. *New York Times,* May 14, 1964, p. 37.

in that case would mean the effort to impose upon the East, then upon Anglicans and the whole Protestant world, her own definition and understanding of the term, regardless of the totality of Christian history and religious experience and the promise of a future level of moral and spiritual life hitherto unattained anywhere in Christendom. In lieu of stuffy arguments over Reformation and Post-Reformation ideas of the nature of the church, too often trimmed to fit contemporary political requirements, there should be a fundamental review of the whole question from the double standpoint of the New Testament, i.e. Christian origins, and the totality of the church's history from the beginning. Far from the appeal to history being "treason," it is the only sound appeal. What has Catholicity actually meant, historically, to Rome, to Orthodoxy, to Anglicans, to Protestants, to Liberals, and to any other Christian group? This inquiry must come first.

There are many fields where we hope the Council will take a stand, for "their voice has gone out into all the world" and will be the most effective statement of the Christian position men have heard for many a year. The Roman Catholic hierarchy in the United States issues a pastoral letter each year, not to Roman Catholics only, but to the whole nation; and it is read with great care and widespread approval. The influence of the bishops reaches far beyond the confines of their own denomination. This will be true of the Council, in a vastly multiplied degree. And we are confident that if the bishops are given the opportunity—or take it—their dealing with our common problems will be constructive, influential, and indeed powerful. I need not here go into these various questions, but they are obvious: Communism (they avoid the word,

and refer to Materialism, Atheism, or antagonism to religion); food production and distribution on a world-wide
scale, not solely for profit; birth control or family planning,
in view of the "population explosion" that is now upon us
everywhere; the armament race; the "crime wave" that
now encircles the globe; the treatment of foreign mission-
aries, especially in "Catholic" countries where they are
unwelcome (at least to Roman Catholics), and by the same
token the designation of "titular sees" in the East, as if
Rome still controlled them; and mixed marriages. These
are practical matters, and need to be handled with charity
as well as understanding, and in a pastoral spirit, as Pope
John admonished. One hesitates to offer suggestions, though
they have been requested. Indeed, as I have said, before the
observers went to the Council, Pope John requested that
we should not confuse observation with journalism—perhaps
recalling what evil irresponsible journalism had wrought in
1869 and 1870, during the First Vatican Council. But everyone knows that the majority of the Council Fathers are
aware of these problems, and are sure to deal with them.
Some proposals that have been made are of a kind that
cannot be withdrawn without action: for example, the
statement on religious liberty, and the repudiation of the
charge against the Jewish people that they "killed Christ."
It is impossible that the Council will fail to act upon these
proposals. To fail to act would result in the strongest vote
of lack of confidence the church could possibly suffer.

The considerations that I have ventured to offer spring
from genuinely high hopes for the future actions of the
Council, as the eventual outcome of the deliberations of the
Fathers. It will, I believe, be an outcome of spiritual renewal, deeper faith, more serious concern for the actual
life of mankind, the widespread and involved problems of

morals, even the economic entanglements of private and family life today. Such old problems as infallibility can either be explained away ("just like the United States Supreme Court, which simply defines what the law is and intends") or quietly shelved and left to innocuous desuetude—it is altogether too limited in scope, when the whole world is crying out for leadership and action.

The results of the Council thus far have been encouraging, few as they are. Everyone knows that the first schema to be approved has been the one on the Sacred Liturgy. Further good results are bound to follow from this decree. Its adoption will be welcomed by almost all Christians, and by many others. There is surely no danger in proclaiming the gospel in a language people can understand, viz. in their mother tongue. That has been the way it has been proclaimed from the beginning. As an ancient Rabbi said, "The Holy One [God] speaks the language of the children of men." And yet there must be reserve, certainly in the choice of the passages from holy scripture to be read at public worship. There are some passages that ought never to be used, passages that reflect all too faithfully the morals of paganism, barbarism, even savagery. There are passages that reflect the violent and bitter anti-Semitism of the first and second centuries. There are others that represent the powerful infusion of Gnosticism, and the reaction against Gnosticism, during the same period—passages composed in order to prove the reality of Christ's human nature and his physical body, as against the Docetists for whom he was only a phantom (cf. Luke 24.37, 1 John 4.2-3). Such proofs are not needed today. In fact, prior to 1945, when a large collection of Gnostic documents was found at Nag Hammadi in Egypt, or rather prior to 1947 when the immense flood of discussion among scholars began, no one suspected the amount and range of Gnostic material there is to be found in the New Testament. It came in from the pagan world surrounding the early church, and it very naturally influenced in some degree the language and thought of nascent Christianity—just as, for example, the "social" emphasis influenced Christian hymnology between 1880 and 1910. But even the anti-Gnostic arguments are now *de trop*.

Fifty or sixty years ago, arguments were advanced to show that early Christianity derived its sacraments from the "mystery religions" that were sweeping over the Graeco-Roman world from the Near East. These arguments were answered as best they could be answered at that time, but both the attack and the defense were feeble. As time has gone by, the probability of some influence, great or small, from the pagan mysteries has become as undeniable as the influence of Gnosticism. The language of the Institution of the Lord's Supper is strongly anti-Gnostic (i.e. anti-Docetic), as it is recounted in the Synoptic Gospels. It is also tinged with a "mystery" conception of the church's sacrament, especially in Mark. John has no account of the Institution, but his language in Chapter 6, especially verses 53-7, is vigorously anti-Docetic and also "mystery" in tone: *trōgōn mou tēn sarka* means literally "gnaw my flesh." To many persons nowadays this language is simply unbearable, explain it how we will, or even volatilize it into metaphor. But Docetic Gnosticism called for such language, if its preposterous view of Christ's human nature was to be ruled out: Gnostics conceived him as a wraith-like "spiritual" being who came and went and disappeared without leaving a trace (John 8.59b, 12.36b). In the *Acts of John* (§93) the disciple testifies that at the Last Supper he put out his hand to touch Jesus, as he reclined beside him, and that sometimes he was there, at other times the disciple's hand passed through the impalpable phantom! It was like the Greek hero in *Odyssey* XI embracing his mother in the underworld—she was only an intangible wraith. Such views need no refutation today, and the use of the language once adopted to refute them adds a further burden to faith, already struggling with the change in world view and the conception of the nature of things forced upon us by modern science.

A further objection is that no Jew could possibly have used such language as "eat my flesh" or "drink my blood." The Jews' horror at the thought of eating human flesh or drinking blood, human or other, forbade the use of any such terms, even metaphorically. Moreover, as every pastor knows, there are many persons who simply cannot bear the thought of partaking of human flesh and blood, however transubstantiated or "spiritualized." Some have told me that they were nauseated by the thought. It was probably Paul who substituted "body" for "flesh" in the church's teaching on the Resurrection (1 Cor. 15), though "flesh" continued to be the language of the creed long after; *resurrectio carnis* in the primitive Apostles' creed of ca. 150 survived for a long time, even as late as the fourteenth century Anglo-Saxon creed, with its *agenrisyng of the flessh.* "Flesh," not "body," continued to be the term used both of the resurrection and of the sacramental Body of Christ in many documents of the early centuries, chiefly anti-Gnostic writings. But Paul did not hesitate to use "body" in his account of the Last Supper in I Corinthians 11.23-6. The relation of the two terms in the early church traditions cannot now be made out, though they certainly reflected variant interpretations, influences *pro* and *contra* Docetism, and even different translations, perhaps, of the original tradition. How far back this tradition can be traced is debated: some scholars doubt if it can have existed in the earliest period, when Aramaic was the language used, not Greek or Latin. The Aramaic word *gûfî* is possible, but does not convey the meaning wanted. The supposition that Paul could have used "flesh" is ruled out by the fact that for him the flesh is the seat of sin, the center of the corruption of human nature, the source of man's opposition to God and His righteousness.

An alternative "canon" is found in the *Didache*, chapter 9. It *is* a canon, for it begins, "Concerning the Eucharist, you are to give thanks as follows." It is reflected elsewhere, and cannot be set aside as a late forgery or creation of fancy: it is biblical through and through.

First concerning the Cup: We give thanks to thee, our Father, for the Holy Vine of thy servant David, which thou didst make known to us through thy Servant Jesus. To thee be the glory for ever and ever. And concerning the broken Bread: We give thee thanks, our Father, for the life and knowledge which thou hast made known to us through thy Servant Jesus. To thee be the glory for ever and ever.

As this broken bread was scattered upon the hills, but was gathered together and became one [loaf], so let thy church be gathered together from the ends of the earth into thy Kingdom, for thine is the glory and the power through Jesus Christ for ever and ever.

But let none eat or drink of your Eucharist except those who have been baptized in the name of the Lord [Christ]. For concerning this the Lord said, "Give not that which is holy to the dogs."

It is only a preconceived dogmatic theory of liturgical history that refuses to view the *Didache* as a genuine early document. Christ not only is but dispenses the Bread of

Life, as also in the sixth chapter of the Gospel of John. It is a figure, as much as "flesh" and "blood" are in the later canons, but it is just as true a figure and historically more probable; for many Christians it is far more significant, as the great hymns and their history and use clearly indicate. Matthew Arnold's *East London* is not modern, but it reflects a stage in religious thought: his friend was "much cheered by thoughts of Christ the Living Bread." It is Christ the Living Bread, the Bread of Life, for which the world is hungering, not his spiritual "flesh and blood." The trend is perfectly obvious in the modern hymnals, books of prayers, and devotional works. For example, the gruesome hymn by poor old William Cowper (1770), beginning

> There is a fountain fill'd with blood
> Drawn from Emmanuel's veins,
> And sinners plunged beneath that flood
> Lose all their guilty stains

—that hymn is almost never heard in Protestant churches today. Yet the old language is still deeply embedded in Christian devotion. The *Anima Christi* is a case in point. Its line, *Sanguis Christi, inebria me* ("Blood of Christ, intoxicate me"), is very antique: the idea, if not the words, could have been borrowed from the cult of Dionysus or of Attis. Or, if the verb was understood in the sense of "drench," it could have echoed the *taurobolium*, possibly as an attempt to outbid and supplant the pagan sacrament— and a great advance upon it, both in idea and in rite. But does it mean that to anyone today? And there are other difficulties. The old translation of *Pange lingua gloriosi* contained a line (Part I, stanza 4) that read: "[whoever

partakes of this sacrament] must from carnal thought be
free." I have known men who were kept from the Holy
Communion by this forbidding statement, which could not
be explained away. The new Episcopal Church hymnal,
The Hymnal 1940, revises it to read:

> ... when man partaketh,
> Though his senses fail to see,
> Faith alone, when sight forsaketh,
> Shows true hearts the mystery.

The new effort sounds somewhat Zwinglian, and seems not
quite Anglican or Catholic in doctrine, but it is a great
improvement upon the old translation. One might wonder
why it was not enough simply to say one must from
"earthly" or "worldly" thought "be free." But the first
thing to inquire is the meaning of the original: this was
not Zwinglian or Anglican but Scholastic. The hymn was
written by St. Thomas Aquinas for the Corpus Christi
festival in 1263; and what he wrote was *Et si sensus deficit*
(as in our new hymnal version). Back of that line is the
usage of the Church Fathers, especially St. Augustine, with
their strong infusion of Neoplatonism, which of course was
some centuries later than the New Testament. At all events,
the demoralizing ambiguity of the unhappy fourth line
(I wonder who composed and inserted it!) in the older
translation is to be avoided at all costs—and that for a pastoral reason, not dogmatic or philological or poetic or any
other, but pastoral, the "cure of souls."

One hopes that the Council will not too hastily do away
with the use of Latin in the Canon of the Mass, or with
the *secreta*, which are a safeguard, and that the words of
administration will continue to be said in Latin (they are

still retained under the new Constitution on the Sacred Liturgy: the words are simply *Corpus Christi*, "Body of Christ"). The rubric *profert verba consecrationis secrete, distincte et attente* ought to have been retained and observed by every Christian church. The problem I have discussed (the words of the Institution) is surely coming up, so far as it relates to biblical research, before the century is out, and will certainly be debated at length. The church will safeguard its most sacred moment of communion with the Risen Lord if it retains the ancient manner of consecration. How old it was, and how impressive to all, Christians and non-Christians alike, is well depicted in Walter Pater's *Marius the Epicurean*, who noted the increasing "mysticity" of the rite. It was the most sacred mystery of the church, and it deserved to be surrounded with every safeguard against profanation and commonness, or misconception and ridicule. One even hopes the Council will not too speedily adopt the proposal of Communion in Both Kinds, i.e. the administration of the Cup to the laity. There are still sound reasons, medical, aesthetic, and devotional, for communion in one kind only.

At the same time, let us hope that the ancient music of the Mass will be retained, and its glorious hymns, for example the sublimely simple Easter Sequence, with its untranslatable *Dic nobis, Maria, quid vidisti in via* (the translation, "Tell us, Mary, what you saw as you were coming along" will never do—it is not poetry!). Or take the sublime *Tantum ergo* (which does have a good English translation), or the majestic *Dies irae dies illa*, which is simply "That day is a day of wrath," based on Amos 5.18-20, with none of the jolly, rollicking lilt of the modern translation, "Day of wrath, O day of mourning." Surely these cannot be altered, revised, satisfactorily translated, or omitted. The testimony of the German bishops at Session I, who reported that where permission had been given to sing vernacular hymns the response was hearty, and at once carried over to the enthusiastic singing of the Latin hymns, is evidence that the case for the Latin hymns is not hopeless. The music of the church is often fully as important as the lectionary, or the sermon, or the public catechism, or the conduct of missions and retreats. If one would hear the church's music at its best, and realize its full teaching and devotional value, making us aware of God's presence and bowing us down in adoration before the Most High, let him go to one of the great churches of the Liturgical Movement, where Gregorian is sung perfectly, and where the congregation takes its full part in the service. Let him go, for example, to Sant' Anselmo, the church of the famous Benedictine monastery on the Aventine, where the music and the liturgy are blended in a perfect harmony of spoken words and song. Here, in this plain and simple rite, with its unadorned ancient ceremonial, its primitive simplicity and directness, its sublime "plain chant" inherited from centuries long past, the divine pledge is fulfilled and our Lord is present "amid two or three," or amid hundreds, and is known to them once more "in the breaking of the bread." It is here, in the profound simplicity of this act of worship, that we begin to realize what fellowship in the united, or reunited, church of Christ can be.